Geoffrey Alderman

THE FEDERATION

OF SYNAGOGUES

A New History

2018

THE FEDERATION OF SYNAGOGUES
A NEW HISTORY

First published in Great Britain 2018 by the Federation of Synagogues

British Library Cataloguing in Publication Data

A catalogue record for this book is available from the British Library

ISBN: 978-0-9934670-3-5

Printed and bound in Great Britain by
Lulu.com

The Federation of Synagogues
65 Watford Way, Hendon, London NW4 3AQ United Kingdom
www.federationofsynagogues.com

TABLE OF CONTENTS

IMAGE CREDITS

PREFACE

In 2014 I was invited by the newly-elected President of the Federation of Synagogues, Andrew Cohen, to revise and update my official history of the Federation, which had been published to coincide with its centenary in 1987. This offered me an opportunity to revisit some of the judgements I had come to at that time, as well as to incorporate the fruits of research – by myself and others – that had been published in the intervening quarter-century.

My centenary volume was not the first history of the Federation. That had been published in 1912 (under the title *The Minutes of the Federation of Synagogues*) and had been written by Joseph Blank, the then Secretary; as I observed in the Preface to my 1987 history, Blank's book is, in truth, nothing more than a chronicle, a highly selective reproduction of extracts from the minute books. In 1937 the Federation asked Dr Cecil Roth (who was later to be one of my teachers at Oxford) to write another history (*The Federation of Synagogues 1912-1937*); but what Roth produced was nothing more than a pamphlet in hard covers, and what he wrote amounted to a sweeping superficiality. Meanwhile, in 1922, the then Sexton of the Federation's Burial Society, Rabbi A. Goldstein, had published a history of the Federation in Yiddish (*Zichron B'Sefer: A Short History of the Federation of Synagogues (London) and its Burial Society*). This volume is in fact shorter by a few pages than Roth's history, but its gossipy style and unashamed bias make it a joy to read. Finally, in 1974, Julius Jung, who had succeeded Blank as Secretary, published under his own auspices a volume entitled *Champions of Orthodoxy*. This book consists in the main of biographical material that had first appeared in the Federation's periodical *Hamaor*; it is a mine of information, collected by an obvious enthusiast and expert who did, however (in my view) suffer from an obvious propensity to exaggerate personal strengths and to minimise personal weaknesses.

In writing my own account of the Federation, I have tried to avoid the stodgy selectivity of Blank, the parochial sensationalism of Goldstein, the whitewash of Roth and the rose-coloured spectacles of Jung. The Federation has certainly had a colourful and controversial past. But I have done my best to put this past in a firm historical context and in this regard I think it worth quoting the opening sentences of the Preface to my 1987 history:

> *The writer of an official history labours under peculiar difficulties. While forming his own independent judgment of the events he portrays, and of their comparative importance, he must nonetheless bear in mind the audiences for whom he is writing. He must never, of course, sacrifice objectivity. Yet at the same time he is ever mindful of the expectations of his clientèle.*

In updating my earlier volume I have dared to hope – as I did in 1987 – that I have written something of interest to the members of the Federation (of which I am one) but also to wider Jewish and non-Jewish audiences.

The major archives of the Federation, from its foundation until the late 1980s, are now housed and expertly conserved in London Metropolitan Archives, Clerkenwell. Those from *circa* 1988 onwards remain at the Federation's Hendon headquarters. Both sets of archives consist of minute books (both of the Council, the Burial Society and of meetings of the Honorary Officers) and associated correspondence files. I wish to place on record (as I did in 1987) my thanks to the present Honorary Officers for permitting me virtually unfettered access to these records. I must also pay tribute to a succession of recent Heads of Administration and Chief Executives (Gerald Kushner, 1989-99; Gordon Coleman, 1999-2006; Dr Eli Kienwald, 2008-2014; and Rabbi Avi Lazarus, appointed 2014) for the expert and painstaking manner in which they have created and preserved these essential collections.

I am grateful for the assistance I have received from Mrs Eve Polikoff, the Federation's former Property Manager and Mr Noson Kahler, the present Sexton of the Federation's Burial Society. A special thanks go to Mrs Judy Silkoff, the Federation's Chief Operating Officer, who has expertly overseen the production of the present volume.

I have benefited immeasurably from conversations with a number of individuals, including former Presidents Arnold Cohen (now deceased) and Alan Finlay, and former Vice-President and Chief Executive Dr Kienwald. A number of other individuals agreed to discuss aspects of the Federation with me on a non-attributable basis. Their knowledge has saved me from many errors and significant omissions. I alone am responsible for any that remain.

As ever, my dear wife has proved a great support and source of inspiration and (most important of all) a good listener. I bless her, and our children, daughter-in-law and granddaughter, and I ask Him from whom all blessings are derived, and to whose Glory generations of loyal Federation members have devoted so much, to deal kindly and with mercy upon all the *Chevrot B'nai Yisroel* ("Societies of the Children of Israel"), wherever they may be.

University of Buckingham   Professor Geoffrey Alderman

29 *Menachem Av* 5777
21 August 2017

ABBREVIATIONS

JADRK   Jewish Association for the Diffusion of Religious Knowledge

JREB   Jewish Religious Education Board

LBJRE   London Board of Jewish Religious Education

CHAPTER ONE

In the Beginning

The first Minute Book of the Federation of Synagogues records that on Sunday 16 October 1887 a meeting of members of so-called "minor" synagogues and *chevrot* (societies; singular *chevra*) in the East End of London took place at the Spital Square Synagogue, Spitalfields. The venue was within the Whitechapel parliamentary constituency then represented at Westminster by a prominent Liberal Member of Parliament, a merchant banker of great wealth, a supporter and friend of the Liberal leader W. E. Gladstone, and a practising Orthodox Jew: Samuel Montagu. It was Montagu who presided over the Spital Square meeting, at which the following resolutions were passed without dissent:

> *That it is desirable for the Chevras to become Federated for certain clearly defined objects.*

> *That a representative of every Chevra or Minor Synagogue in East London be invited to attend a preliminary meeting to be held at the Spital Square*

Synagogue on Sunday, November 6th, at three o'clock, to discuss plans for a Federation of the Chevras.

And so, on the duly appointed afternoon, representatives from eighteen synagogues met, again under Montagu's chairmanship, to formally constitute themselves as a new organisation in Anglo-Jewry, the Federation of Minor Synagogues.

It was determined that the Federation would be managed by a Board of Delegates, which met for the first time on Sunday 4 December. At this meeting, sixteen synagogues were represented. The largest, Sandys Row, boasted some four hundred members, whilst the smallest (Carter Street and Mansell Street) had barely four dozen between them. Indeed, the total membership of the founding synagogues did not exceed about 1300, whereas the total Jewish population of Great Britain at that time was probably about

Samuel Montagu, Lord Swaythling, 1900

a hundred times that figure. But the founders of the Federation knew that, though small in numbers, they nonetheless represented a movement of profound importance to the Anglo-Jewish community, and one whose significance could never be measured simply in numerical terms. Had not Nathan Mayer Rothschild, undisputed lay leader of British Jewry (recently elevated to the peerage as the first professing Jew to be a member of the House of Lords) consented to become the Federation's President? More than that, Rothschild had found time to preside in person at the Board meeting held on 16 January 1888, to see for himself what this Federation was about. In truth, the Federation was anything but "Minor", an epithet that was soon dropped from the formal title.

In order to understand how the Federation came to be established – and why – we must put its Minute Books to one side and look instead at the complex mosaic of Anglo-Jewish communities in the later decades of Queen Victoria's reign.

In the decade of the 1880s, Anglo-Jewry had found itself in a state of turmoil. Since the readmission of the Jews to England, which Oliver Cromwell had sanctioned in 1656, the community had grown to about 60,000, of whom over three-quarters lived in London. The original Sephardi community based upon the Bevis Marks synagogue in the City of London had been overshadowed, first in numbers and later in wealth, by an Ashkenazi community which, by the 1880s, boasted no less than a dozen major places of worship. The oldest of these (and the largest in terms of male membership) was the Great Synagogue, Duke's Place, Aldgate. In 1870, a private Act of Parliament had permitted the Great Synagogue to amalgamate with its two close neighbours, the Hambro' and the New, and with two 'branch' synagogues – the Central (controlled by the Great) and the Bayswater (controlled jointly by the Great and the New) to form the United Synagogue, to which, in due course, other Ashkenazi congregations, such as the St John's Wood, the East London (Stepney) and the Dalston had been admitted.

The United Synagogue had been established, in part, to act as an instrument of communal control. The founding fathers of the United Synagogue all came from families of great substance and standing, such as the Rothschilds and the Cohens (descendants of Levi Barent Cohen, whose numerous offspring had married into the houses of Rothschild, Montefiore and Samuel). A grandson of Levi Cohen, Louis Cohen, had been instrumental in persuading the London Ashkenazi congregations to appoint one "Chief Rabbi", Dr Nathan Marcus Adler, elected to that office in 1845, and it is clear that this demonstration of communal co-operation was a prelude to the formal union of 1870. In that union Louis Cohen's son, Lionel, had played a prominent part.

The Cohens were successful stockbrokers and bankers. Louis lived, in a style commensurate with his wealth, in Gloucester Place, Marylebone, where he kept a strictly Orthodox household, and where he entertained other well-to-do Jewish businessmen. Amongst these was Samuel Montagu, who had moved from Liverpool (where he had been born on 21 December 1832) to London to establish a private banking firm in the City. Montagu, too, was strictly Orthodox. Gratified, no doubt, to find that the Cohens of Gloucester Place observed the Sabbath with meticulous care, he was happy to accept their hospitality, and became a frequent visitor. In March 1862 he married Ellen, one of Louis Cohen's daughters, and so was formally admitted (so to speak) into membership of 'the Cousinhood' – Anglo-Jewry's ruling elite of mega-wealthy, inter-related families. In this way one of the founders of the United Synagogue and the founder of the Federation were already brothers-in-law long before either institution had been formally constituted.

Those who established the United Synagogue had been motivated by the firm conviction that the growth of London Jewry out from the City into the suburbs needed to be supervised and controlled, partly (it was said) to ensure the maximum and most economical use of communal resources, but partly also to guard against schismatic tendencies. The secession of eighteen

Sephardim and six Ashkenazim in 1840, to form the West London Synagogue of British Jews – the first Reform synagogue in the United Kingdom – was an experience that none of the lay leaders of Anglo-Jewry wished to see repeated: it was a challenge to their authority (particularly that of Sir Moses Montefiore, who as President of the Board of Deputies of British Jews had refused to admit to membership of the Board any Jew who was an adherent of the Reform movement) and it was an encouragement to others. In this respect the installation of Nathan Adler as Chief Rabbi possessed an importance that was much more than symbolic.

Born in Hanover in 1803 and, at the time of his election, *Oberrabbiner* of that city, Adler was, without any doubt, a man of great Jewish learning, the author of a number of works of Talmudic scholarship, of which *Netina la-Ger*, a commentary upon the Targum Onkelos, was the most celebrated. As Chief Rabbi in London, he could claim an allegiance which his predecessors could not, for his was the first election to that office in which provincial communities had been invited and encouraged to participate as well as the London Ashkenazi congregations. Adler believed – to the evident relief and satisfaction of the Ashkenazi lay leadership – that the Orthodox structure in England was too weak to permit the growth of genuinely self-governing communities, as existed in Germany, Poland and Russia, each with its own *Beth Din* (Rabbinical Court) and its own, independently regulated, communal infrastructure. In England (Adler believed), what was needed was the firm centralisation of religious institutions, under his aegis.

Nathan Adler was not blind to the general and growing laxity that existed within Anglo-Jewry as far as religious observance was concerned, and he did what he could to rectify matters. In particular, he resisted for as long as possible the efforts of members of synagogues under his control to modify religious services along Reformist lines. His success may be measured in one of two ways. On the one hand, we are justified in pointing to the fact that under Adler's spiritual guidance the United Synagogue remained firmly

Orthodox in its theology and in its self-identification. On the other, we must note that the liturgical modifications to which he was persuaded to agree in 1880 were said to have been partly responsible for his virtual retirement from the Chief Rabbinate that year. It does seem evident from his own writings that Nathan Adler regarded Orthodoxy within the Anglo-Jewry over which he presided as, if not exactly a lost cause, certainly an exceedingly weak one. In 1888, from his retirement in Brighton, he addressed an impassioned circular to his rabbinical colleagues in Eastern Europe, begging them to prevail upon their congregants "not to come to the land of Britain for such ascent is a descent".

Nathan Adler died on 21 January 1890, a little more than two years after the Federation had been established. He was succeeded by his son, Dr Hermann Adler, who had in fact been acting as "Delegate" Chief Rabbi for the past decade. Hermann possessed neither the intellectual stature nor the religious confidence of his father, and proved unequal to the enormous strain to which events elsewhere were now subjecting Britain's Jewish communities.

Viewed from the perspective of world Jewry, Britain was, in the mid-19th century, a backwater. Certainly as far as the Ashkenazim were concerned, the epicentre of the Jewish world and of the Jewish people was to be found in western Russia, Russian Poland and Austrian Poland (Galicia), in which areas lived over four million Jews, whose undeniable material poverty was balanced by an intensity of religious life with which that in England simply did not bear or merit comparison. Under successive Tsarist regimes the lives of Jews in the greater Russian empire had become increasingly miserable. But the assassination of Tsar Alexander II, in 1881, opened a new and much more horrific chapter for them. A wave of officially inspired pogroms spread across the Pale of Settlement in Western Russia. The attacks were renewed and intensified between 1882 and 1889, when the impoverished Russian peasantry found an outlet for their discontent in gratuitous anti-Jewish violence. There was a further wave of pogroms between 1902 and 1906. Meanwhile, Jews in

Poland and Galicia had begun to move westwards in search of a better life. The trickle of Jewish migrants from Eastern Europe before 1880 became a flood thereafter.

This great migration was destined to change the face of British Jewry and especially of London Jewry. Most of the migrants thought in terms of immigration to the United States of America – the *Goldene Medina* ("Golden Land"), where so many of Europe's refugees and dispossessed had built new lives. Relatively few Jews thought of permanent settlement in England, which was merely a stopping place on the way to America, a point of arrival at Grimsby, Hull or Tilbury, a cross-country train journey, and then a point of departure at Liverpool or Southampton. Sometimes, however, the emigrant's cash ran out: he could reach England but could go no further until more money had been earned and saved. More often, a sojourn in England that was intended to be temporary became permanent settlement. The artisans and craftsmen and women, the tailors, dressmakers, glaziers and furniture-makers who journeyed westwards found that they could exist – just – by working exceedingly long hours and living, as immigrants newly-arrived in England have always lived, in the poorest and most squalid parts of the great cities. In London, this meant the "East End".

No-one supposed that the life was pleasant; it wasn't. But it was free from persecution and terror and, however meagre the financial rewards, there was economic opportunity of a sort, some hope of advancement, whereas in the Pale of Settlement there had been none at all. There was also an established, well-to-do Jewish community that had clearly made its way in the gentile society that surrounded it. This fact itself gave grounds for optimism. Whatever their motives, between 1881 and 1914 some 150,000 Jews from Eastern Europe settled in the British Isles. London Jewry, which numbered about 45,000 in 1880, increased three-fold by the turn of the century. The existing community was swamped by the newcomers. A demographic and, as it turned out, a social and religious revolution was under way.

This is not the place to examine in any detail the anti-Jewish prejudices triggered by this great influx. But it is necessary to refer to them, and to bear them in mind, in order to appreciate more fully the strained relationship between the old, established Jewish community and the new. The Jewish immigration coincided with the end of "the mid-Victorian boom" and the onset of an economic depression. As unemployment deepened, immigrants inevitably found themselves singled out as a major cause of the sharp downturn in trade and industry. The most intense phase of this "anti-alien" legislation was not inaugurated until May 1901, when Major William Evans-Gordon, the newly-elected Conservative MP for Stepney, helped found the British Brothers' League. Four years later the League scored a remarkable political victory when it persuaded A. J. Balfour's government to pass the Aliens' Immigration Act, a thinly disguised attempt to halt the flow of Jewish refugees into Britain.

That the Act was supported by a number of Jewish Members of Parliament, including Harry Samuel (MP for Limehouse), Louis Sinclair (Romford) and Benjamin Cohen (Islington), President of the Jewish Board of Guardians (whose task it was to care for the Jewish poor) gives us a clue as to the attitude of the Anglo-Jewish gentry towards their less fortunate brethren from Eastern Europe. When we remember that at the general election of 1900 both Evans-Gordon and another notorious anti-Semite, David Hope-Kyd (who had unsuccessfully contested the Whitechapel seat against Samuel Montagu's nephew, Stuart Samuel) had both had the official support of Lord Rothschild, the President (it will be recalled) of the Federation, we can be left in no doubt that, with a few exceptions, the Anglo-Jewish establishment viewed the mass migration of Jews to this country with a calculated antipathy, in which Chief Rabbi Hermann Adler fully shared: for he, too, refused to condemn the 1905 legislation.

The prime cause for concern was the effect which the influx of thousands of Jewish pauper immigrants was bound to have upon the status, standing and image of the Jewish communities already settled in the UK, and the agitations to which their presence was bound to give rise. The political emancipation of British Jewry had only been fully secured in 1858, when Lord Rothschild's father had secured the right of professing Jews to be elected to and take their seats in the House of Commons. His epic struggle was well within the memory of those who led the community, and the United Synagogue, in the 1880s. They remembered, in particular, that the battle had been won on the grounds that the Jewish subjects of Queen Victoria differed from her non-Jewish subjects only in respect of their religious observances. But it was now undeniable that the majority of Jews living in Britain and in London were "aliens". As the *Jewish Chronicle* (28 September 1888) put it:

> *If poor Jews will persist in appropriating whole streets to themselves in the same district, if they will conscientiously persevere in the seemingly harmless practice of congregating in a body at prominent points in a great public thoroughfare like the Whitechapel or Commercial Road, drawing to their peculiarities of dress, of language and of manner, the attention which they might otherwise escape, can there be any wonder that the vulgar prejudices of which they are the object should be kept alive and strengthened?*

It caused little surprise, therefore, that the Board of Guardians advertised in the Jewish press in Russia and Romania that Jews who sought to escape persecution by coming to Britain would face many hardships, and would certainly not obtain relief from the Board during the first six months of residence – when they needed it most! Those migrants who did reach Britain were encouraged to continue their journeys (to America or South Africa), and some were indeed persuaded to return whence they had come.

These policies reflected the outlook of the leading families in Anglo-Jewry and of the communal institutions they controlled. But their views were not universally shared. There were individuals in the community whose attitude to their unfortunate brethren was more in accord with traditional Jewish values, and who clearly felt themselves – certainly from a religious point of view – closer to the new arrivals from Eastern Europe than to the Anglo-Jewish establishment.

Among these were Hermann Landau, Ellis A. Franklin and Samuel Montagu.

Hermann Landau (1844 – 1921), whom we shall later meet as a founder and, in time, a Vice-President of the Federation, was himself an economic migrant. He had been born in Constantinow, in Russian Poland, and had emigrated to Britain in 1864, eventually becoming a wealthy stockbroker. Landau had had a traditional Jewish education, and was not ashamed to call himself a "Polish Jew" even though he lived in the West End of London. Ellis Abraham Franklin was, like Montagu, a bullion broker and had, in 1853, joined the firm of Samuel Montagu & Co; in 1865 he married one of Montagu's sisters, and became his business partner three years later.

Hermann Landau, 1900

Montagu himself was, by the 1880s, an acknowledged authority on financial matters, the head of an exceedingly successful banking firm that specialised in currency and bullion dealings on an international scale. His business affairs had brought him into contact with foreign governments and British politicians, who sought his expert advice. Montagu was a man of vast wealth, which he enjoyed using for philanthropic purposes, and both Jewish and non-Jewish causes benefitted from his munificence. He was also a Radical – that is to say, his political views lay on the left wing of the Liberal party then led by W. E. Gladstone, and at the general election of 1885 he had won the Whitechapel seat for the Liberal party after a campaign that was blatantly 'Jewish.'

For the next fifteen years, therefore, the parliamentary constituency most thickly populated with Jews was represented by a Radical politician who could address his co-religionists in the one language they all spoke and understood – Yiddish – and who was, moreover, as utterly and uncompromisingly

Montagu Family, 1905

Orthodox as they could have wished. For it was well known that Montagu observed all the minutiae of the requirements of Orthodox Judaism, both in his public and private life. In this respect Montagu was a model Jewish MP, combining a deep involvement in public affairs with an equally deep and abiding religious faith that underpinned his entire outlook. In her biography of her father, published in 1913 (at page 18), his daughter Lilian had this to say of him:

> *The religion of Samuel Montagu affected his whole conception of life. He was a Jew primarily — and a citizen, a politician, a business man long afterwards. It was with Jewish eyes that he judged men and things.*

We should not be surprised that this pillar of *Yiddishkeit* held radical views. His radicalism, and especially his conviction that the rich had a duty to help the poor, sprang from his deep knowledge of Orthodox Jewish ethics. He lived, in palatial splendour, at 12 Kensington Palace Gardens, and he owned a large country estate at Swaythling, near Southampton. But he recognised that the bonds which linked him to the Jewish poor of London's East End were eternal, and he rejoiced in them.

In 1885 a series of events occurred which brought into very sharp focus the differences that existed – certainly on the subject of Jewish immigrants - between the Rothschilds, Montefiores and Mocattas on the one hand, and Hermann Landau, Ellis Franklin and Samuel Montagu on the other. These events formed an immediate backcloth to the foundation of the Federation of Synagogues.

Early in 1885 the attention of the Jewish authorities in London was drawn to the activities of Simon Cohen, a pious Jewish emigrant from Poland who, having settled in England in 1870, had established himself as a prosperous baker in Aldgate. *Simha Becker* (as he was affectionately known) interested himself in the plight of his fellow Jews who arrived at the docks with little if any money and very often without the slightest idea where they might find lodgings, let alone any means of employment. It was feared that in this condition they might become an easy prey to Christian missionaries, who were known to wait at the dockside and to offer food and shelter to those who would go with them, and also free medical aide, none of which was to be had from the Jewish Board of Guardians. Simon Cohen was appalled at this state of affairs and – without bothering to ask the permission of the Anglo-Jewish grandees – arranged (in 1879) for premises at 19 Church Lane (which lay between Commercial Road and Whitechapel Road) to be used as a hostel for Jewish immigrants. In surroundings which were certainly austere the immigrants were assured of shelter, clothes, kosher food and even facilities for prayer and religious studies. Bread which Cohen had not managed to sell by the end of the day was divided between the inmates of his "Shelter" and the Salvation Army, which William Booth had established in the East End at about the same time.

Simon Cohen became a folk-hero. In a modest fashion he disbursed modest charity, without the formalities or restrictions imposed by the Board of Guardians, but with a warmth and fellow-feeling that the immigrants at once recognised. It was for these very reasons that the Anglo-Jewish authorities determined to put a stop to his activities. In April 1885 Frederic Mocatta, a Vice-President of the Board of Guardians, accompanied by Lionel Alexander, the Board's Honorary Secretary, visited the Shelter and pronounced it "unhealthy"; they further reported that "such a harbour of refuge must tend to invite helpless Foreigners to this country, and therefore was not a desirable institution to exist." (Minutes of the Board of Guardians, 13 April 1885). The authorities in Whitechapel were prevailed upon to have the Shelter closed.

This precipitate action backfired – and spectacularly so. Mocatta was obliged to appear and defend the policies of the Board of Guardians at a protest meeting held at the Jewish Working Men's Club & Institute, Whitechapel. The Club (at which, in its early years, meetings of the ruling bodies of the

Federation were to be regularly held) had been established (probably on the initiative of Chief Rabbi Nathan Adler) in 1874. It had grown out of The Jewish Association for the Diffusion of Religious Knowledge, of which Samuel Montagu had become President in 1869, and it was Montagu who headed (with a donation of £600) the list of contributors to a fund which enabled the Club to open substantial purpose-built premises in Great Alie Street in February 1883. Montagu quickly distanced himself from the policy of the Board of Guardians in relation to Simon Cohen's Shelter. The premises were undoubtedly cramped and overcrowded but the services provided therein were, in Montagu's view, absolutely necessary.

More worrying, however, were the daily signs of the ever-deepening alienation of the newer immigrant Jewish community from the established leadership. In commenting upon the affairs of the Shelter, the *Jewish World* had given public expression to these fears:

> *We are sorely afraid that the wisest steps have not been taken in reference to the Home for the Outcast Poor in Church Lane. The very establishment of the Home and its unaided maintenance by the poor themselves is sufficient to show that something of the kind is required, or, at least, that there is a strong feeling among the foreign poor that it is required. To meet such a feeling by an abrupt contradiction is only calculated to precipitate the hostility towards the recognised channels of communal relief, which has been fermenting for some time among the foreign portion of the East End community.*

Hermann Landau had already reached a similar conclusion. He opposed the continuation of the Shelter, on the grounds that its activities would encourage the establishment of a Polish-Jewish ghetto, which – as an anglicised Polish Jew – he naturally viewed with some distaste. But he did favour (so the *Jewish Chronicle* reported on 15 May 1885) "an institution in which newcomers, having little money, might obtain accommodation and the necessaries they required at cost price, and where they would receive useful advice".

Landau, Franklin and Montagu therefore became the sponsors of a new and more formalised establishment, which opened its doors at 12 Great Garden Street in November 1885, and which was known as the Poor Jews' Temporary Shelter; Franklin was its President (to be succeeded, later, by Landau), and Montagu its Treasurer. This Shelter, which subsequently moved to 82 Leman Street, served two meals a day, gave no financial assistance, and did not allow anyone to remain under its roof for longer than two weeks. Even so, the Board of Guardians refused for fifteen years to become reconciled to it, demanding (*inter alia*) that it should only admit adult males and that those who did not find work after leaving the Shelter should be referred to the Guardians for

IN THE POOR JEWS' TEMPORARY SHELTER.

For the bulk of the people I have

'The Poor Jews' Temporary Shelter

repatriation. To these conditions those who managed the Shelter absolutely refused to adhere.

In this way Montagu and his friends openly repudiated the policies (and therefore, to some extent, the authority) of the ruling circles within Anglo-Jewry in the early 1880s. However, Montagu's differences with the leadership on matters pertaining to the immigrants were not limited merely to the question of poor relief. The most obvious and deepest gulf that divided the immigrants from the establishment was not financial, but religious. And in matters of religious observance Montagu was drawn instinctively towards the viewpoint of the immigrants rather than to that of the United Synagogue.

Some reference has already been made to the state of religious observance within Anglo-Jewry at this time. With the appointment of Hermann Adler as Delegate Chief Rabbi in 1880, British Jewry acquired as its acting spiritual head (at least as far as Ashkenazim were concerned) a man who, though born abroad (in Hanover, in 1839), had been educated in England before obtaining his doctorate in Leipzig in 1862 and his rabbinical diploma (*Semicha*) in Prague the same year. Hermann felt himself to be totally English; his sermons were models of elegant Victorian prose; he was also a capable administrator. Although, therefore, unlike his father he made no original contribution to Jewish theological exposition, he was well liked by anglicised members of the community, with whom he enthusiastically identified himself.

Hermann Adler made no secret of his desire to meet the wishes of those within the United Synagogue who favoured yet more modifications to its liturgy. He adopted Anglican clerical garb, complete with gaiters, and styled himself "The Very Reverend", the form of address used of Deans of the Church of England. Moreover, although occupying the office of Delegate and, later, of full Chief Rabbi, he insisted for many years upon maintaining the fiction that there were no other rabbis in the land over whom he could be "Chief", for he would not allow it. In this matter he followed the ruling of his father, who would neither grant the rabbinical diploma to any other minister of religion within the United Kingdom, nor allow the title of "Rabbi" to be used by those who had gained such diplomas abroad, as the Adlers had done. This absurd rule – a product of Adlerian vanity and authoritarianism – was not relaxed until 1901, when Hermann agreed that examinations for the diploma might henceforth take place, under his chairmanship, at Jews' College.

In this matter, perhaps more than any other, Hermann made himself an object of ridicule in the eyes of the Jewish migrants who flocked to Britain from Eastern Europe after 1881. He persisted in addressing as "The Reverend Mr" outstanding rabbinical scholars such as Avraham Aba Werner, the famous rabbi of the Spitalfields Great Synagogue, the *Machzike Hadass* ("Upholders of the Religion"), and Eliezer Gordon, founder of the Yeshiva of Tels, in Lithuania. But the insult Hermann Adler offered to sages of this calibre was not merely personal, or based upon some idiosyncratic protocol. In refusing to accord equality of status with himself to religious leaders who stood (if truth be told) head and shoulders above him in terms of Talmudic scholarship and piety, Adler sought to impose upon the immigrants the reality of his undisputed religious leadership. The failure of such a policy was entirely predictable.

The Jewish emigrants who came to London in the late 19th century examined the religious institutions which operated under the aegis of the Chief Rabbi, and found them woefully deficient. To begin with, the very idea of a "Chief Rabbi" was viewed with suspicion and mistrust. In Poland and Russia every community had its own rabbi, whose duty it was to supervise the various activities necessary to the community's well-being, such as *shechita* (the Jewish humane method of slaughtering food animals) and the authorisation of marriages. The status of one rabbi as compared with that of another would depend entirely upon the communal view of their respective rabbinical abilities. Matters of dispute would be settled by the local *Beth Din* (rabbinical court), upon which would sit three or more *dayanim* (judges), appointed on the basis of their sagacity and religious reputation.

Under Hermann Adler, by contrast, the whole of the United Kingdom (indeed, the entire British Empire) had only one "Rabbi" – himself – who proudly cultivated the appearance of a Christian cleric and whose religious Orthodoxy was open to question. Even in the time of Hermann's father, the *Beth Din* in London had only one permanent *dayan*, Aaron Levy, who had retired in 1872. Within a few years the *Beth Din* had been taken under the wing of the United Synagogue. Bernard Spiers was appointed a *dayan* in 1876, but did not enjoy the confidence of the immigrants. The appointment as *dayan* of rabbi ("reverend") Ya'acov Reinowitz was more sympathetically received, and *sha'alot* (questions pertaining to religious matters) were invariably referred to him for detailed scrutiny. But the presence upon the *Beth Din* of only one person who had the full confidence of the religious community merely served to underline its lack of status.

In any case, Hermann Adler made it abundantly clear that he did not consider himself bound by its authority. In accepting the position of Chief Rabbi in his own right, following his father's death, he had intimated (in a letter to the Secretary of the United Synagogue, 23 November 1890) that he would not agree even to be obliged to consult the *Beth Din*, and that "The visitation of Provincial Synagogues and Schools is exclusively the function and duty of the Chief Rabbi, as is the visitation of a diocese by its Bishop," (quoted in A. Newman, *The United Synagogue*, p.94). Nothing could have encapsulated more eloquently Adler's view of his own position in Anglo-Jewry. It was a position that the immigrants of the 1880s and 1890s totally rejected.

But it was not only the religious organisation of British Jewry that the newcomers found objectionable. The synagogue buildings erected and maintained by the United Synagogue were large cathedral-like structures, built to accommodate many seat-holders at rentals which very few immigrants could have afforded, and totally lacking in the intimacy and atmosphere of the synagogues in the Pale of Settlement. To the vast majority of English Jews the synagogue was a place of formal worship, nothing more. To the immigrants it was a social institution, most certainly a place for prayer (though without the assistance of a choir), but also a place for contemplation, for the study of Talmud, for the discussion of communal problems.

It was within the framework of the synagogue that benefit societies were established to provide for those who fell on hard times and, in particular, to make payments to mourners during the period of seven days' confined mourning (*shiva*) immediately following bereavement, when no work is allowed. Even when the recipient was not a member of a society, or had technically fallen out of benefit, the disbursement of such monies was not regarded as mere charity, but as a religious duty – *gemillat chassodim* ("acts of loving-kindness"). Those who had, unfortunately, to ask for such support knew that their cases would be considered by people who were, in all probability, their friends and neighbours, and who would be well acquainted, therefore, with their personal circumstances: embarrassment was reduced, if not eliminated altogether.

When the immigrants arrived in the East End they naturally wished to preserve and rebuild these societies (*chevrot*) and, equally naturally, they sought out those who came from the same areas, often the same towns, in central and Eastern Europe, to help in this task. The synagogues which they established were frequently given names that advertised the geographical origins of their members, such as the Grodno Synagogue (44 Spital Street), the Kovno Synagogue (Catherine Wheel Alley), the Warsaw Synagogue (Gun Street, Spitalfields), the United Brethren of Konin Synagogue (84 Hanbury Street), the Brothers of Petrikoff Synagogue (Sly Street). The names of other synagogues reflected the particular purpose of those who had established them: the Sons of the Covenant Friendly Society (Hope Street); the Holy Calling Benefit Society (16 New Court, Fashion Street); the *Chevra Kehol Chassidim* ("Society of the Community of the Pious", 5 Old Montagu Street). Others, again, simply expressed an ethical principle, or contained a Biblical reference: the Glory of Jacob Synagogue (18 Fieldgate Street); the Peace and

Truth Synagogue (Old Castle Street); the Love and Kindness Synagogue (Prescot Street).

In this connection we should note that the very term "synagogue" is misleading, for it conventionally denotes a purpose-built or purpose-rebuilt structure dedicated to Jewish worship, whereas a quorum of ten males above the age of thirteen is all that is required for Orthodox Jewish prayer. Such an assembly may be constituted in any suitable room, or even in the open air. In a few cases the immigrants in the East End were able, in the course of time, to acquire imposing structures in which to worship and study: in 1898 the *Chevra Machzike Hadass*, formed in 1891, obtained the sub-lease of a beautiful Huguenot church at the corner of Brick Lane and Fournier Street, which was known thereafter as the Spitalfields Great Synagogue.

The history of the *Machzike Hadass*, and of its epic struggle with Chief Rabbi Hermann Adler over the lamentable standard of kashrut which Adler permitted in relation to the supply of kosher meat and poultry, do not, strictly speaking, belong to that of the Federation of Synagogues. Nonetheless we should bear in mind that those who founded this community were in the mainstream of immigrant disenchantment with the established institutions of Anglo-Jewry even though, in rebelling as they did and in establishing their own shechita, they went much further than most of the immigrants were, at that time, prepared to go. We should also note that the Spitalfields Great Synagogue applied to become affiliated to the Federation on 9 July 1901.

Most *chevrot* could not afford spacious premises for their meetings, but made do with a room or rooms within the complex of garment workshops where they worked, or else built makeshift structures in the yards adjoining the tenement buildings in which they dwelt. The early minutes of the Federation contain some vivid descriptions of such synagogues. On 19 January 1897 the Federation's Building Committee reported that it had visited the *Chevra Mishnayot* at 16 Church Lane, "but could not get admission. It was ascertained that the Synagogue is held in a large room on the second floor, and that there are only forty members". Of the *Chevra Kehol Chassidim* at 35 Fieldgate Street the Committee reported:

> *This Chevra numbering 52 members has been in existence eight years, and recently came into possession of the Synagogue at 35 Fieldgate Street. It partakes of the character of a Beis Hamedrash being open all day for study. The members contributed 5d [five old pence] a week, the income aggregating to about £100 per annum. There is a mutual benefit fund; loans being advanced free of interest. ... The synagogue is approached through a somewhat dingy passage, and is built in the same way as many workshops in the locality, on what was originally the open space at the back of the house. There are between 80 and 90 seats for males, and no provision for females.*

On 13 May 1900 the Board of the Federation heard the following report from its Honorary Architect (Lewis Solomon) concerning an application (subsequently rejected) for affiliation from the Kurland Synagogue, 133 Cannon Street Road:

> *There is no accommodation for women ... the building is not such as to command respect ... it is unsafe from a fire point of view, as if a fire occurred in the house there would be a panic in the synagogue & possibly not a soul could escape unhurt.*

While it was obviously desirable, from the point of view of health and safety, to replace such accommodation with specially constructed synagogues, most *chevrot* were in no position to afford such luxury and, without Samuel Montagu's intervention, would not have been in such a position for a very long time. In any case, when the immigrants came to London the erection of synagogues was not their major priority.

In matters of religious observance one of their overriding concerns was to provide or have access to a properly-consecrated burial ground. The United

Synagogue had several, and was prepared to allow burial of non-members, but at fees which most immigrants could not afford. In those cases where fees were not paid, burials were still carried out (as is required by Jewish Law), but in unmarked graves, upon which no tombstones might be erected until all outstanding charges had been settled.

The early minutes of the Federation reflect the obvious preoccupation of the immigrants with this distressing state of affairs. In July 1888 the United Synagogue agreed to reduce the charge for a "second class" funeral to £3, but was adamant in refusing to lower the charge for children's funerals. In order to assess the impact of this policy we need to bear in mind that infant mortality was then far higher than today. The records of the Federation's own Burial Society, established on 15 April 1890, show that during the first two years and eight months of its existence it carried out 199 interments, of which (including stillbirths) no less than 117 were of children under one year old. It is, therefore, not merely a matter of record that the Federation was not founded as a Burial Society; we might speculate, indeed, that had those who led the United Synagogue at that time shown greater compassion, this aspect of the Federation's work might well have been deemed unnecessary.

The anguish of parents who could not afford to bury their children touched Samuel Montagu very deeply. But he was as disturbed as the Anglo-Jewish establishment by the unwelcome publicity which the immigrants were attracting to themselves, and which appeared to threaten the image of British Jewry in its entirety. An aspect of this problem which Montagu viewed with particular concern was the socialism and militant trade-unionism that some of the immigrants brought with them. They came to England from societies in Eastern Europe which, though enclosed, were nonetheless rich in political and industrial organisation. In towns such as Vilna (Lithuania) and Vitebsk and Gomel (Belarus), trade unions flourished, at least for a time, at the end of the 19th century. Many of these unions owed their inception to socialist activists, and many devoutly Orthodox Jews experienced no inner conflict when they repaired to their synagogues for religious services three times each day and then used the same premises to discuss socialist principles and to organise industrial stoppages.

The immigration from Eastern Europe created a Jewish proletariat in the East End of London, and one, moreover, which was fully prepared to give a platform to socialist propagandists. When a Jewish socialist organisation had first appeared in the capital (Aaron Lieberman's Hebrew Socialist Union, at 40 Gun Street, Spitalfields), in May 1876, Jewish communal leaders acted quickly to suppress it. One avenue of attack was to persuade Zvi Hirsch Dainow, a popular Russian *maggid* (preacher) recently arrived in England, to deploy his oratorical powers against the socialists. Lieberman's Union broke up of its own accord, however, and its founder left England to pursue revolutionary activities in Vienna and Berlin. But in 1879 his disciple, Morris Winchevsky (the alias of L. Benzion Novochovitch) arrived in London to carry on his work. Winchevsky had attended the famous Vilna Yeshivah and was able, in his writings, to summon up a rich variety of religious images. He was also an accomplished journalist. On 25 July 1884 he and a friend, Elijah Wolf Rabbinowitz, founded the first socialist newspaper in Yiddish, *Der Polisher Yidl* ("The Little Polish Jew").

The socialism of *Der Polisher Yidl* was, however, implicit rather than explicit. Much of its content was focussed on the plight of East End Jews, and it was not above taking the Jewish workers themselves to task for indulging in vices such as gambling. Rabbinowitz was determined not to allow his politics to interfere with his commercial judgment: his acceptance of religious advertisements annoyed Winchevsky, and the partnership fell apart when an election advertisement was accepted from Samuel Montagu. In the pre-history of the Federation this incident is of some importance. It demonstrated, on the one hand, how closely involved Montagu was with the social dynamics of the Jewish East End: he was prepared to advertise, in Yiddish, in what was really a very small circulation journal, read by people who for the most part did not enjoy British voting rights. On the other, however, it also illustrated the antipathy of Winchevsky and his comrades to Gladstonian Liberalism. On 15 July 1885 they brought out the first issue of the *Arbeter Fraint* ("Worker's Friend"), the declared aim of which was "to spread socialism among Jewish workers"; it remained the major Yiddish socialist newspaper in Britain for the next decade.

The rise of the *Arbeter Fraint* alarmed the leadership of Anglo-Jewry, including Montagu, to a far greater extent than had the activities of Aaron Lieberman a decade previously. The Hebrew Socialist Union had never been anything more than a tiny band of semi-intellectuals. The *Arbeter Fraint* made its appearance at a time of great depression in the British economy. The mid-Victorian boom had come to an end, and there was much resultant distress: riots of the unemployed took place at Hyde Park in February 1886 and at Trafalgar Square in November 1887. In 1884 a group of revolutionary socialists, led by H. M. Hyndman and including the celebrated textile designer and political activist William Morris, had founded the Social-Democratic Federation, of which an East End (and in practical terms Jewish) branch was in the course of time established. Devotees of the *Arbeter Fraint* themselves organised a Society of Jewish Socialists (1884), out of which grew the International Workers' Educational Club, with premises at 40 Berner Street, off the Commercial Road. In 1886 the Berner Street Club (as it was popularly known) took over publication of the *Arbeter Fraint*. It inevitably became a rival of the Working Men's Club in Great Alie Street and served as the meeting-place for every sort of radically orientated Jewish immigrant in London. It also helped stimulate contact between Jewish workers and British socialists, for it was visited by a succession of left-wing personalities, including Hyndman and Morris.

The spectre of Jewish participation in a socialist movement in Britain was cause enough for anxiety – even though (as events turned out) the immigrants were for the most part far too busy keeping body and soul together to worry about social revolution. To the Jewish masses in the East End, as elsewhere in

Britain, socialism meant little as an ideology, though much as a framework for industrial organisation: the small band of Jewish social-democrats and anarchists found that they were in demand not as political agitators but as trade-union managers. However, national attention had already been focussed upon the immigrants in a context which was derived wholly from their status as an alien and exploited proletariat, and which demanded an official Anglo-Jewish response.

In March 1884 the medical journal *Lancet* began publishing reports by its "Special Sanitary Commission" on the condition of Jewish immigrant workers in the UK. Four years later both Houses of Parliament began investigating all aspects of immigration, while the Board of Trade conducted its own inquiries into the sweating system in Leeds and the East End of London. These initiatives triggered a public debate about Jews, the Jewish way of life and the effect which Jewish immigrants were said to be having upon the standard of living of those in whose midst they now dwelt. The young Beatrice Potter (later Mrs. Sidney Webb), then working with the celebrated social investigator Charles Booth in his comprehensive survey of the *Labour and Life of the People of London* (published 1889), noted that the Jews were regarded as "a race of producers with an indefinitely low standard of life". While admitting that the Jews were law-abiding, she felt that they were prepared to engage in competition "unrestricted by personal dignity of a definite standard of life". The Jewish immigrant, she concluded, "though possessed of many first-class virtues", was nonetheless "deficient in that highest and latest development of human sentiment – social morality".

In fact, the allegations that the Jews deprived their English-born neighbours of work, by accepting lower wages and tolerating a generally inferior standard of life, were without foundation. The immigrant Jews were as much the victims of cut-throat competition as anyone else but – pre-eminently in the garment trades – they actually created new employment opportunities. Yet, however ill-informed and malevolently motivated, the hue-and-cry directed against the Jewish immigrants frightened the Anglo-Jewish leadership, who were prompted to try to put their own house in order without government interference.

One way of doing this was to promote the formation of non-socialist trade unions, whose major task it would be to ensure that existing factory legislation was enforced in the sweatshops. In 1884 the *Jewish Chronicle* urged the Board of Guardians to undertake such a promotion, but the Guardians were in truth much too closely identified with the Anglo-Jewish ruling elites to be taken seriously in this regard. Samuel Montagu had a much better chance of success. As the MP for Whitechapel and already closely involved with the life of the immigrants, he knew from first-hand experience how assiduous were socialists (Jewish and non-Jewish) in exploiting work-place and social grievances for political ends. Already known as a labour arbitrator and patron of the Jewish Working Men's Club, Montagu achieved further popularity in immigrant circles by founding (1886) and supporting the Jewish Tailors' Machinists Society, whose (unsuccessful) aim it was to achieve a maximum working day of twelve hours without recourse to the strike weapon.

Montagu feared socialism not so much in a religious sense (though the atheism that characterised so much of the socialist leadership was anathema to him) but because of the bad name which he felt would accrue to Anglo-Jewry through the activities of socialists within the immigrant community. The *Jewish Chronicle*, which Montagu owned jointly with Lionel Louis Cohen and Lionel Van Oven, had for some time been stressing the necessity of anglicising "the foreign contingent", which it saw as "the great task before the London Jewish community" (11 February 1887). The *chevrot*, the *Jewish Chronicle* had declared, "originate partly in the aversion felt by the foreign poor to the religious manners and customs of English Jews. The sooner the immigrants to our shores learn to reconcile themselves to their new conditions of living, the better for themselves. Whatever tends to perpetuate the isolation of this element in the community must be dangerous to its welfare." (23 January 1880). Two weeks later the *Jewish Chronicle* was even more strident in its tone:

> *To form 'wheels within wheels,' or little communities within a great one, is to weaken the general body. They have no right, if permanent residents, to isolate themselves from their English coreligionists ... They should hasten to assimilate themselves completely within the community amongst whom they dwell.*

There were calls at this time, and subsequently, for the *chevrot* to be federated, a move that Hermann Adler himself favoured. However, nothing was done until, in February 1887, an event occurred which galvanised the Anglo-Jewish leadership and confronted it with the need to take action to counter socialist penetration of the *chevrot*.

The socialists had begun to adopt an Irish tactic, that of using funerals for propaganda purposes. They issued an invitation, in Hebrew, to the Jewish workers of the East End, calling upon them to attend "the funeral [at the United Synagogue's West Ham cemetery] of our comrade Simon Sweed, boot-finisher, 26 years of age, who fell a victim to the present system of production". This prompted Montagu and Frederic Mocatta to make a heavy-handed attempt to suppress the *Arbeter Fraint* by bribing the printer and compositor to sabotage its production. The stratagem misfired, for within three months the paper had acquired its own printing press and was back on the streets. Public disquiet at the presence of the immigrants was, moreover, gaining fresh momentum. In April 1887, at the Assembly Hall, Mile End Road, the anti-Semitic propagandist Arnold White had called a meeting to urge an official inquiry into "the immigration of foreign paupers". Montagu, who appeared on the platform, defended the Jews but felt he could not oppose the inquiry which, as we have noted, Parliament launched the following year.

Montagu and his friends felt that they needed to be able to supervise the affairs of the immigrants, who now comprised three-quarters of London

Jewry, and in particular to demonstrate that the newcomers comprised a well-ordered, law-abiding, non-socialist element within Anglo-Jewry. At Berner Street, Montagu was persona non-grata. But in the *chevrot* it was a different matter. As a leading member of the Anglo-Jewish gentry Montagu was no schismatic. He did not wish to see the immigrants erect and maintain a set of communal institutions that would be independent – entirely beyond the control or even influence of those already established. But from a spiritual point of view he was well able to understand why the immigrants wished to have little to do with the establishment, and in this respect he sympathised fully with their outlook.

At the founding meeting of the Federation of Synagogues Montagu and Hermann Landau both emphasised their determination not to interfere with the rules and customs of the *chevrot*. Montagu made it clear that his objectives in inaugurating the Federation, were to counter the anti-immigrant agitation, to present a united front, and to show that the Jewish immigrants were be no means socialists and republicans. "Although there might be one or two Socialists," he told the meeting, "these were quite the exception to the rule."

Those who led the United Synagogue hoped that the *chevrot* could be stamped out. The minutes of the United Synagogue's Council for 18 February 1890 record its view that:

> *At a time when the desire of the community is to unite as much as possible*
> *its various organisations ... it surely seems inopportune to create and extend*
> *a body whose policy must inevitably tend to disunion and disintegration.*

Montagu's approach was much more realistic. The members of the *chevrot* would not join the United Synagogue, and any attempt to force them to do so would lead to a complete break, which would mean, in effect, the repudiation by what had clearly become the majority of London Jewry of the authority and status of the established community. This authority and status could best be preserved and (he admitted frankly) the less desirable features of *chevrot* life (such as its openness to socialist propaganda, and the proliferation of very small, unsafe synagogue premises) could best be brought under control by providing the *chevrot* with a communal framework of their own which would leave them with a reasonable amount of autonomy in religious affairs, but which would, at the same time, bring them within the ambit of the already-existing communal organisation.

Hermann Landau, in a letter published in the *Jewish Chronicle* on 24 May 1889, put the matter more bluntly:

> *In the latter part of 1887 great dissatisfaction was expressed in the East End with existing ecclesiastical arrangements and meetings were actually held to organise a new Shechita Board, etc. The Federation was called into existence to prevent any development of this movement, and has, therefore, been the means of preventing communal disunion.*

The motives of Montagu and his friends in sponsoring the establishment of the Federation seem clear enough. Of Montagu himself it has sometimes been said that he desired to supplant Lord Rothschild as the undisputed lay leader of Anglo-Jewry and that the launching of the Federation was designed to achieve this end. This was certainly the view spread by gossip-mongers at the time. But there is not a shred of evidence to support it. At no time did Montagu ever use his unassailable position within the Federation for his own personal or private ends.

What of the immigrants themselves? Why did the *chevrot* agree to become 'federated'? The deeply-felt matter of funeral costs has already been touched upon. We should remember too that, as aliens, with little immediate prospect of naturalisation (the fee for which was beyond the means of most recently-arrived immigrants), they lived each day in fear, if not of deportation, then certainly of a change in government policy that might well prevent their relatives and friends from joining them in the UK. The unity provided by the Federation, and the sympathetic ear of a prominent member of the House of Commons and – what is more – of a fellow orthodox Jew, were valuable assets. We must not suppose that the immigrants enjoyed worshipping in cramped and often wholly unsuitable premises: Montagu's money promised many improvements in this regard. Finally, the immigrant Jews wanted status and recognition. As members of many small *chevrot* they were totally excluded from representation on any of the communal institutions, such as the London Board for Shechita (of which Montagu was President) and the Board of Deputies of British Jews; nor were their synagogues recognised by the civil authorities for marriage purposes.

The *chevrot*, in short, wished to have some voice in the policy-making organs of Anglo-Jewry. Forming themselves into a Federation, under the leadership of Samuel Montagu, seemed to be the easiest and most practicable way of achieving this end.

CHAPTER TWO

Early Development

The "minor" synagogues whose representatives attended the foundation meeting of the Federation were not all of recent origin, for invitations had also been sent to a number of small congregations which had not been included in the United Synagogue scheme of 1870. No less than three of these *chevrot* dated back to the 18th century. The oldest was the Prescot Street Synagogue, founded in 1748; the Carter Street Synagogue had been established in 1790; and the Scarborough Street Synagogue traced its origins to 1792. Five other congregations predated the immigration of the 1880s. The Sandys Row *chevra* had been founded by working-class Dutch immigrants in 1851; the consecration of its place of worship, in 1851, had been snubbed by Chief Rabbi Nathan Adler. The *Chevra Bikur Cholim* ("Society for Visiting the Sick") in Fashion Street and the German Synagogue in Spital Square (which played host to the foundation meeting) both traced their origins to 1858, as did the Fashion Court *chevra*. The Princes Street *chevra* dated from 1870.

These synagogues now joined with eight post-1881 foundations (the "Konin", Hanbury Street; the Marshall Street *chevra*; the "Kalischer" *chevra*; the "Peace &Truth" *chevra*, Old Castle Street; the "Voice of Jacob" *chevra*, Pelham Street; and the *chevrot* in Dunk Street, Windsor Street and Hope Street) in agreeing to form themselves into a Federation to be known in Hebrew as the *Chevrot B'nai Yisroel* (the "Societies of the Children of Israel"), and in English as the Federation of Minor Synagogues. At its meeting on 6 November 1887 the Board of Delegates of the Federation proceeded to frame a constitution, which set out the following "Objects" [objectives]:

I.   To provide or render available to the members of the Federation the additional Services of Jewish Ministers.

The Poltava Synagogue 1925

a. Such Ministers to be the medium between the Federated Synagogues and the established Ecclesiastical Authorities of the Spanish and Portuguese Congregation and of the United Synagogue.

b. To visit at houses for the purpose of promoting the spiritual and physical welfare of East London Jews.

c. To attend and preach at the Synagogues of the Federation, whenever it may be necessary.

II. To endeavour to lessen the number of Charity Funerals by negotiating with the United Synagogue, or with others, for burials at moderate cost.

III. To obtain representation at the Board of Shechita.

IV. To obtain representation at the Board of Deputies.

V. To obtain representation at the Board of Guardians.

The determination of the Federation to become fully involved in the major communal organisations of British Jewry is evident in these objectives. But it is noteworthy that the first of them was subsequently modified to make it clear that any Minister or Dayan appointed would have to be "certified as holding Orthodox opinions, by the Ecclesiastical Authorities". In other words the Federation, in appointing its own spiritual leaders, would acknowledge the primacy of the Chief Rabbi, and would not establish a religious authority in opposition to him.

The constitution also provided for a Board of Delegates, consisting of the President and one elected member from each Federated Synagogue, plus one elected representative "for every whole number of 50 contributing adult male members of each of such Synagogues". Elections to the Board were to take place every two years, and the Board was to meet at least once every month, except August and September. When the Board was not in session the affairs of the Federation were in the hands of an Executive Committee, elected by the Board and consisting of the Presidents of all the synagogues in the Federation, plus the Honorary Officers. At the first meeting of the Board (4 December 1887), the Honorary Officers were elected as follows: President, Lord Rothschild; Vice-President (also known as "Acting President"), Samuel Montagu; Treasurers, H. Landau and I. Weber. A Secretary, Joseph E. Blank, was appointed, at a salary of £20 per annum, "for the period of one year". In fact, Blank was to remain in post until May 1925!

Some other features of the constitution deserve comment. The first is the prominence given to Lord Rothschild. This was not merely a public acknowledgement by members of the Federation of Rothschild's pre-eminence in British Jewry; it was also a public declaration that the Federation, far from having been established in opposition to the United Synagogue, acknowledged its central importance in the affairs of London Jewry. Indeed, at its meeting on 20 January 1889 the Board of Delegates went further, by stipulating "That the President for the time being of the United Synagogue shall be Honorary President of the Federation & shall be invited to attend the Meetings of the Board".

The second aspect of the constitution worthy of note is that nowhere did it provide for the Federation to have an income of its own. The affiliated *chevrot* paid no membership fees, which in truth the vast majority of them could never have afforded. Some synagogues organised collections for Federation purposes, but these were quite voluntary and yielded only small sums. The accounts of the Federation for its first year of existence show an income of £119 and an expenditure of just over £52, leaving a surplus of £66 and 13 shillings. But this creditable result was only achieved after Montagu had himself made a donation of £64. In November 1888 Montagu announced his intention of making over to the Federation, to defray its administrative expenses, the sum of £50 per annum for each of the ten following years.

To put matters bluntly: the wheels of the Federation were oiled by Samuel Montagu's money. At its foundation it is clear that he hoped the wealthier sections of the London Jewish community would contribute to the maintenance of the Federation not by outright gifts, as he was doing, but by giving it a reasonable share of the general funds available for communal use. One important source of such funds was the London Board of Shechita, which had been established in 1804 in order to supervise the slaughter and sale of meat and poultry. The cost of the facilities provided by the Board of Shechita formed part of the overall price charged to customers by the retail butchers whom it licensed, but to this price was added a further sum which has traditionally been regarded as a form of communal taxation. These surpluses, or profits, were distributed each year by the Shechita Board to its "Parent Bodies", the Spanish & Portuguese Congregation and the United Synagogue. The Parent Bodies naturally elected the Board itself, and had the right to nominate its Ecclesiastical Authorities – the Haham (spiritual head) of the Sephardi community, and the United Synagogue's Chief Rabbi.

In March 1888, the Federation secured modest representation (one representative) on the Board of Guardians without difficulty, and Federation synagogues were likewise admitted to the Board of Deputies (the Spital Square synagogue returned one Deputy in and from 1889). But Montagu's hope that the Federation would be admitted without demur onto the Shechita Board, and be allowed (as representing a very large and growing number of consumers of kosher meat and poultry) to share in its profits received an early and ominous setback.

Montagu, as President of the Shechita Board, appears to have believed in November 1888 that he had obtained the agreement of the Sephardim and of the United Synagogue to the Federation having three representatives on the Board, and a one-fifth share of its profits. But the United Synagogue was not in fact prepared to tolerate such an arrangement. When the Board's half-yearly distribution of profits took place, early in 1889, the Federation ought to have received £80. It obtained nothing. Montagu thereupon sent the Treasurers of the Federation a cheque for £60 while negotiations with the United Synagogue proceeded. But these proved abortive. Justifying its obstinacy, the Executive Committee of the United Synagogue accused the Federation of enticing away individual synagogues and of refusing to take its proper share of the financial burdens of the community. Each year thereafter Montagu provided the Federation from his own pocket with a sum equal to that which it ought to have received from the Shechita Board until, in January 1899, the United Synagogue relented and agreed to allow the Federation to participate in the Board's activities. In February 1901, after having been made to wait for twelve years, the Federation received its first remittance from the Board of Shechita, a cheque for £76.

The dispute of 1888-89 over the right of the Federation to share in the activities and profits of the Shechita Board paralleled that, to which reference has already been made, concerning the refusal of the United Synagogue to lower its burial fees. Members of Federation synagogues were prepared to be patient in regard to the Shechita Board; but the matter of burial demanded an early solution. In January 1889 Montagu announced that he had acquired, at a cost of nearly £1,000, two acres of land from the Western Synagogue cemetery at Edmonton, Middlesex, "in the name and for the use of the Federation", and that he had reserved within this new burial ground a double plot for himself and his wife. A committee was elected to draw up a scheme of administration. The resulting Laws and Bye-Laws of the Federation Burial Society were adopted by the Board of Delegates in February 1890. They provided, *inter alia*, for a voluntary *Chevra Kadisha* ("Holy Society") to carry out the sacred rites pertaining to the preparation of the dead for burial, and for membership of the Burial Society to be available to members of all Federation synagogues at a subscription of one-and-a-half [old] pence per family per week.

Since these monies were collected via the synagogues, membership of a synagogue or *chevra* affiliated to the Federation now carried with it a valuable privilege. By 1891 the Burial Society numbered 600 male members, though (as with any newly-established insurance fund) it was not yet self-supporting. In July 1891 the Federation was obliged to vote it a grant of £50. But by 1893 it had reached the stage of financial independence, having recorded a surplus of income over expenditure of £16. On 24 January 1896 Montagu informed Joseph Blank that he had decided to make over to the Burial Society a gift of a further three acres of land at Edmonton. This land adjoined the cemetery of the independent Maiden Lane Congregation, which had become defunct. In 1908 the Federation Burial Society purchased this cemetery and incorporated it into its own Burial Ground. In due course further land at Edmonton was acquired. By 1912 the Federation Burial Society had on its books nearly 5,000 male members (representing perhaps four or five times that number of persons), belonging to some fifty synagogues. It also had a cash reserve of over £4,000, and could now afford to contribute to the finances of the Federation: the previous year it had made the first of a series of annual donations of £100.

Edmonton Cemetery

Montagu's munificence extended well beyond even these very considerable gifts. From time to time he made over to the Federation blocks of Treasury stock ("Consols"), which could be sold at a handsome profit. He also gave very substantial sums towards the building or rebuilding of synagogues, in a manner which fulfilled a number of purposes at once. Although Montagu wished to see the *chevrot* flourish, he did not favour the proliferation of many small, insanitary and unsafe synagogues. In 1890 it was decided that every synagogue affiliated to the Federation should be brought up to certain minimum standards on the recommendation of the Honorary Architect, Lewis Solomon. Those whose premises were found to be deficient were given loans to enable improvement to be carried out, and others were admitted to the Federation only on condition that specified improvements were effected. Some (such as the Kurland Synagogue, Cannon Street Road) were refused admission; their members were advised to transfer to other congregations, or to combine with others to build "model" synagogues. The first of these, the New Road Synagogue, close to the London Hospital, was opened by Lord Rothschild on 24 May 1892.

Where loans were granted the money did not come from the Federation but from Montagu himself, who generally stipulated that the capital was to be repaid to him in agreed instalments, but that the interest was collected by the Federation. On 15 November 1889 the *Jewish Chronicle* reported that during the first two years of its existence Montagu's gifts to the Federation had exceeded £2,000; to this should be added a loan of £300 which he made to one *chevra*, and the £300 per annum salary which he paid to the Federation's Minister, Dr Lerner.

In 1889 relations between the Federation and the United Synagogue reached a new level of hostility. The United Synagogue accused the Federation of enticing away individual congregations: The Federation, though ostensibly an "East End" body, had admitted into membership the New Dalston *Chevra*, Birkbeck Road, but a United Synagogue congregation was already in existence in the area. There were, in truth, two Jewish communities in Dalston, one of which had been drawn quite naturally to the Federation's side. A deeper cause of tension was the alarm felt in United Synagogue circles that Montagu's Federation would perpetuate the separatism of the *chevrot*, and not assist in their absorption into what was regarded as the mainstream of Anglo-Jewish life. In February 1888 Lord Rothschild had written to the Federation undertaking "on the part of the United Synagogue, that that body will in no way seek to interfere with the Federation except to advise it in such matters as affect Jews generally". But within the space of two years this policy had given way to one of outright hostility.

New Road Synagogue c1940–c1949

In January 1890, the United Synagogue's Executive Committee published an ambitious plan to erect in Whitechapel a "properly conducted Synagogue", capable of seating 1,200 persons, and to reinforce the *Beth Din* by appointing to it "a gentleman who, through his intimate knowledge of the habits and customs of Polish and other Foreign Jews, will possess the necessary qualifications for the combined office of Dayan and Preacher". The "proposed Colossal Synagogue" (as Montagu called it), to be subsidised by non-residents at the rate of £1,000 per annum, was rightly regarded as an attempt to put the Federation out of business. In a letter published in the *Jewish Chronicle* on 15 January 1890 Montagu warned that "The Jews of Whitechapel desire to control their own Synagogues", and that they would not desert their "small and numerous" places of worship for the proposed gargantuan edifice. He was right. The agitation for the United Synagogue's East End Scheme abated, and though it was revived at various times in the 1890s, the Colossal Synagogue was never built.

Instead, the United Synagogue embarked upon a more modest scheme of synagogue building in north and north-west London, hoping to attract those immigrants who were already beginning to move out of the East End. The Federation responded by encouraging the formation of affiliated congregations in these and other areas. Charges and counter-charges of 'poaching' were unfortunately to become a feature of relations between the two communal organisations. On 24 May 1899, the Federation's Burial Committee complained that "at extremely short notice the Sandy's Row Synagogue left the [Burial] Society, having made an arrangement with the United Synagogue ... by the bait of lower subscriptions". Later that year Montagu reported that he had acquired, at a cost of £1,500, a freehold building suitable for a Federation synagogue in the Notting Hill district, where a constituent of the United Synagogue had functioned since 1879; the Federation synagogue was consecrated by the Chief Rabbi in 1900. By 1911 synagogues affiliated to the Federation were to be found also in Stoke Newington, South Hackney, Limehouse, Canning Town, Bow, Tottenham, Walthamstow, Woolwich and

Plumstead. In all, the Federation at that time represented about 6,500 male members. It had, therefore, overtaken the United Synagogue (which then had about 5,200 male seat-holders in membership), and could rightly claim to be the largest synagogal body in the United Kingdom.

We have already noted that the first "Object" of the Federation, as expressed in its Constitution, referred to the desirability of appointing Ministers to provide for the spiritual needs of affiliated congregations. Being totally independent, and in control of its own affairs, each of these congregations was at liberty to appoint a Minister for itself, and a number of *chevras* did in due course acquire the services of eminent rabbis. Among these may be mentioned David Rabinowitz and Moshe Avigdor Chaikin at the "Peace & Truth" synagogue, Old Castle Street; Eliyahu Shalom Regensberg and Ya'akov Dimovitch at the *Ain Ya'akov* ("Well of Jacob") *chevra*, Artillery Lane; Pinchas Ya'akov Gerber of Cannon Street Road; Yehuda Leib Levene of Little

Cannon Street Road Synagogue, 1930

Alie Street; Shmuel Kalman Melnick of Princelet Street; and the renowned Avraham Aba Werner of the Spitalfields Great Synagogue.

These rabbis dealt with the religious needs and problems of their congregants, by whom they were paid exceedingly modest salaries. They were neither appointed by nor responsible to the Chief Rabbi, whom – as we have seen – the immigrants did not hold in high esteem. The *Kulturkampf* between immigrant Orthodoxy and the Judaism of Hermann Adler reached a crisis point in 1891. Having failed to persuade the Chief Rabbi to institute a much more rigorous supervision of butchers licensed by the Board of Shechita, members of the *Machzike Hadass* community established a shechita facility of their own. Whatever sympathy Montagu may have had with the *Chevra Machzike Hadass* was outweighed firstly by his position as President of the Shechita Board and secondly by his determination to stamp out schismatic tendencies in Anglo-Jewry. At the Federation, he was able to have postponed indefinitely moves (November-December 1891) to appoint a committee "to inquire into the prevalent rumours as to the condition of the Kosher Meat as supplied in the East End of London".

Meanwhile, as the dispute dragged on and became ever more bitter, Montagu offered the services of the Federation, and his own financial resources, as a way of bringing matters to a conclusion. In July 1901, the Board of Delegates resolved to admit the Spitalfields Great Synagogue "subject to an assurance being received from Dr. Adler that the Synagogue will conform to his religious authority & to the laws of the land most especially affecting Marriage & Divorce". The Synagogue was formally admitted on 28 February 1905, following confirmation of an agreement between the *Machzike Hadass* community and the Board of Shechita providing for the continuation of the community's shechita under the authority of the Board; at the same time the jurisdiction of the Chief Rabbi was recognised "provided that he acts in accordance with the Shulchan Aruch [Code of Jewish Law]". Upon its admission into the Federation, the Synagogue was given a loan of £1,000, half of which came from Lord Rothschild and half from Montagu.

In this way Montagu and the Federation managed to uphold the authority of the Chief Rabbi and of the Board of Shechita, while at the same time accommodating the religious sensibilities of a most important section of the immigrant community. In its biennial report the Federation put the matter thus:

> *While carefully avoiding recriminative details the Federation may claim that throughout the unhappy secession it has ever been ready to provide the golden bridge for making union and concord ... Such a part the Federation is happy and proud to play, but these sentiments are not unmixed with a sense of its accompanying great and grave responsibilities.*

The issue of rabbinical independence was scarcely less delicate. Since the immigrants had little confidence in the Beth Din of the United Synagogue, they naturally looked to their own rabbis as the ultimate arbiters in religious matters, including marriage and divorce. Sometimes, however, these rabbis were indeed ignorant of the requirements of English law. The United Synagogue itself, in propounding its East End Scheme, had acknowledged the desirability of appointing to the Beth Din a Minister who would have the confidence of the East End Jews. Dayan Reinowitz alone possessed this confidence, but he was already over 70 years of age and in poor health (he died in May 1893), "allowed to subsist [declared the *Jewish Chronicle's* obituary notice] on a miserable pittance grudgingly given by the United Synagogue".

The decision of the Federation to appoint a Minister of its own, whose services would be available to all affiliated synagogues but who would function under the jurisdiction of the Chief Rabbi, was therefore well grounded in the religious needs of immigrant Jews in London. But the circumstances which surrounded the appointment had less to do with purely religious matters than with Montagu's fear of the growing influence of socialists within the immigrant community.

In January 1889 Lewis Lyons, a social-democrat of independent views who had once been a contributor to the *Arbeter Fraint*, assumed the leadership of the East End garment workers, then suffering unspeakably as victims of the system of sweated labour. Lyons and Philip Krantz, the *Arbeter Fraint's* first editor, formed a Committee for Jewish Unemployed and tried to enlist the support of the Delegate Chief Rabbi in their campaign against sweating. On the Sabbath of 16 February 1889 a procession was organised to the Great Synagogue, where Hermann Adler obliged by preaching a sermon against the agitators. On Saturday 16 March a much bigger demonstration was mounted: the unemployed passed a resolution criticising Adler for his refusal to speak out against the sweating system. At the Great Synagogue itself there had been a visible police presence; in the afternoon fighting had broken out at the Berner Street Club, and arrests had been made.

These events horrified the Anglo-Jewish establishment, though not for the reason often given, namely that the Sabbath had been publicly desecrated. Public desecration of the Sabbath was habitually practised by Jewish employers of sweated labour, a fact – unpalatable to some – which the Federation did not ignore. In 1897, on the initiative of the Sabbath Observance Committee, the Board of Delegates resolved "to ask the Chief Rabbi ... to invite the heads of the large Jewish firms who do & do not observe the Sabbath both in the West End & East End to a private meeting & induce the latter to keep that day holy & thereby set an example to their poor brethren & be the means of not compelling them to desecrate that day by employing them to work & keep themselves from starving". As a result of this initiative Adler was prevailed upon to sign, jointly with Montagu, a letter to employers on the subject of Sabbath observance and to appear at the Working Men's Club (10 July 1898) to denounce, jointly with Dayan Susman Cohen (the late Dayan Reinowitz's son-in-law), the widespread desecration of the Sabbath day.

The activities of Lyons and Krantz shocked the establishment for a very different reason, for they appeared to be succeeding in spreading socialist propaganda among the immigrants and, at the same time, in bringing about confrontation between Jews and the police, resulting in very unfavourable and negative publicity. The Federation, whose members included many small employers as well as many workers, faced both ways. There was of course a great deal of sympathy with the workers, whose grievances resulted, in the late summer of 1889, in a bitter strike, of five weeks' duration, for a twelve-hour day, including one hour for lunch and a half-hour for tea. Montagu and Rothschild both contributed to the funds of the strike committee, and Montagu, together with Mark Moses, the employers' leading spokesman and a founder of the Federation, were instrumental in effecting a settlement: the masters agreed to the demands of the men, on condition that the latter did not bring up the question of wages for one year.

At the same time there was genuine concern in Federation circles at the extent of socialist influence. This concern pre-dated the strike, for at a Board meeting held shortly after the March 1889 Great Synagogue demonstration one delegate "called attention to certain socialistic disturbances which had taken place the previous Saturday & said that the Federation, representing as it did the Jews of East London, should disclaim any connection or sympathy with the socialists". Following his successful intervention in the strike, Montagu wrote to Joseph Blank (6 November 1889) in the following terms:

> My experience gained during the recent strike convinces me that the influence of a few Atheists [i.e. socialists] over Jewish Working Men can no longer be ignored. I therefore appeal with confidence to the Federation of Synagogues, comprising so large a number of observant Jews, to take the lead in combating this most serious evil. I propose that the Federation should promptly engage a gentleman well acquainted with Judisch Deutsch [Yiddish] and able to lecture in English as a Maggid, or Minister (not

Dayan), Salary £300 per annum — no perquisites or other gains to be permitted.

Qualifications: To be a Talmudic Scholar, well versed in Jewish Law, Orthodoxy to be vouched for by our Ecclesiastical Authorities; in religious matters he must be under the jurisdiction of Dr. Adler.

Duties: His whole time to be at the disposal of the Council [Board of Delegates] of the Federation. He must not undertake any duties beyond those prescribed by the Council of the Federation. On week days he must devote himself to visiting among the Jews in East London, advising them in case of need and generally promoting the objects of the Federation. On Sabbaths and Festivals he is, if so directed, bound to deliver two sermons daily at Synagogues designated by the Council.

Montagu indicated that, on acceptance of these conditions, he would place in the hands of the Federation's trustees the sum of £900, to cover the salary of the Minister for three years. Advertisements were in due course inserted in the major Jewish newspapers in England, Germany, The Netherlands and New York and, from eighteen applicants, a shortlist of four was drawn up. On 26 January 1890, at a meeting at Great Alie Street intended primarily for the Board of Delegates but actually packed to capacity with excited Federation members and (the *Jewish Chronicle* noted) some members of the Great Synagogue, each of the contenders was required to deliver a sermon of a half-hour's duration. Voting took place by secret ballot and resulted in the election, by 30 votes to 6, of Dr Mayer Lerner (1857-1930), then Rabbi of Wintzenheim, in Alsace.

Mayer Lerner's appointment was without doubt an important milestone in the development of the Federation, though it was not intended – by Montagu – to have the significance it later acquired. Montagu's conditions could not have been clearer: the Minister was not to be a Dayan, for that might have presupposed the establishment by the Federation of a Beth Din of its own, in opposition (it would have been said) to that operated by the United Synagogue under the authority of the Chief Rabbi. Moreover, so as to emphasise the subordinate position of the Minister, he was to function under the Chief Rabbi's jurisdiction.

But on 21 January 1890 – five days, that is, before the dramatic meeting at which Dr Lerner was elected – Chief Rabbi Nathan Marcus Adler had died. The appointment of his son Delegate Chief Rabbi Hermann Adler, as Chief Rabbi in his own right, was regarded as a matter of course; but the United Synagogue was obliged to convene a conference of all congregations contributing to the Chief Rabbi's Fund and, in any case, a decent interval had to be observed between the death of one Chief Rabbi and the appointment of another.

Chief Rabbi Hermann Adler c1905–c1909

The confirmation of Hermann Adler as Chief Rabbi did not take place until 1891. At the conference which elected him the honorary officers of the United Synagogue insisted that the number of delegates allowed to each participating congregation must be proportional to the amount contributed to the Chief Rabbi's salary; this formula had been used on the occasion of Nathan Marcus Adler's election, and it suited the wealthy families who controlled the United Synagogue that it should be applied following his death. The result was that the United Synagogue controlled 218 votes, whereas the other participating bodies were allotted a mere 47 votes in all. In order to obtain representation at the conference the Federation had, in March 1890, agreed to vote £10 to the Chief Rabbi's Fund and was, in May, given to understand that it would be entitled, therefore, to eight votes. Measured against the thousand or so male members then attached to Federation synagogues, such representation would have been derisory enough, but it was later reduced to two votes (both cast by Hermann Landau), a circumstance which led Montagu (April 1891) to enter a vigorous protest on the Federation's behalf.

Thus, the election of Hermann Adler as Chief Rabbi of the United Hebrew Congregations of the British Empire was regarded by many in the Federation with decidedly mixed feelings. East End Jewry had been largely ignored. What is more, Hermann Adler was not required to live in the East End, a condition to which he had categorically refused to be bound. Mayer Lerner, by contrast, resided in Aldgate (46 Great Prescott Street) during the entire period of his incumbency as Minister of the Federation (January 1890 – May 1894) and, though seventeen years younger than Adler, was already a more distinguished rabbinical scholar. Like Adler, he had gained a doctorate from the University of Leipzig, but his Rabbinical Diploma had been conferred by the renowned Rabbi Dr Ezriel Hildesheimer of the *Adass Yisroel* Synagogue in Berlin. He had written a number of scholarly treatises on the origins of parts of the Talmud and, at the time of his appointment to the Federation, had in the press a collection of responsa. In 1886 he had married Henrietta, a grand-daughter of Rabbi Samson Raphael Hirsch, arguably the foremost exponent of the revival of Jewish Orthodoxy in 19th century Germany.

Lerner arrived in London on 26 March 1890 and delivered his inaugural sermon at the Bevis Marks Synagogue of the Spanish & Portuguese Jews' Congregation (there being no Federation synagogue capable of accommodating the large numbers of people who had come to hear him) three days later. From the outset he identified himself with the tribulations and the aspirations of the poor Orthodox Jews among whom he lived, visiting them in their homes and listening to their problems. Lerner did preach against socialists and atheists, but he quickly grasped the essential fact that the maintenance and strengthening of Orthodoxy were crucially dependent upon the religious education given to the young, and it was to this pressing matter that he primarily addressed himself.

Dr. Mayer Lerner c1890-c1895

The Jewish education of the young immigrants then living in the East End, and of the children of immigrant parents, may be briefly summarised:

The Jews' Free School, in Spitalfields, then the largest elementary school in England, catered for about 4,300 children and had a staff of over 70, many of whom were in fact pupil-teachers. The headmaster, Moses Angel, considered the school's overriding task to be the Anglicization of the children in his care; their parents were, in his view (1871) "the refuse population of the worst parts of Europe". The East End also contained some smaller Jewish state-aided ("voluntary") schools: two Jews' Infant Schools, the Stepney Jewish School, and the Spanish & Portuguese School. Together with a few minor institutions these schools accommodated in 1880 about 4,500 children; by 1900 the figure had risen to about 8,000.

But the total number of Jewish children in London at the end of the 19th century was certainly over 21,000. Those – the majority – not fortunate enough to attend a Jewish school were therefore – for the most part - educated in the schools of the local education authority, the London School Board. At Board schools (some of which were composed almost entirely of Jewish children) the Jewish content in the curriculum was provided – if at all – by the Jewish Association for the Diffusion of Religious Knowledge (JADRK). But, poorly supported by Anglo-Jewry, the Association could never manage to provide teachers for more than about a third of the pupils, and the teachers it did provide were often ill-qualified for the task in hand. It was partly in order to fill this gap that the *chedorim* (literally "rooms", usually in a teacher's house) flourished. Here the *melamed* (teacher), usually a religious official such as a shochet or beadle, (and almost invariably without formal training as a teacher) would supplement his other income by endeavouring to inculcate, in surroundings totally unfitted for the purpose, an elementary education in Hebrew and Judaism into children whom he taught before school in the mornings and then again in the late afternoons and evenings. The charge was generally about one shilling per child per week.

The manifest inadequacy of the religious education given to Jewish youngsters struck Lerner within a short time of his arrival in London. In October 1890 he persuaded the Board of the Federation to appoint a committee to undertake a systematic investigation of Jewish education and religious training in the East End. Its printed report, presented on 7 April 1891, remains a masterly summary of the situation, all the more forceful because of the uncompromising way in which it condemned the *chedorim* system:

> *There are considerably more than 200 Chedorim in the East End, where at least 2000 boys from 5 to 14 years of age are trying to learn Hebrew ... in the large majority of cases a bed room or kitchen is used ... sometimes with a sick wife or child in the bed room, with cooking or washing being done in the kitchen. In nearly every instance the surroundings are of the most insanitary description and the teachers in the most abject poverty.*

The Committee also visited schools run by the London School Board. At some, such as Old Castle Street (where 95 per cent of the pupils were Jewish), the JADRK provided Hebrew teachers, but at others, such as Settles Street, "excepting two young pupil teachers, no Jewish teachers are on the staff ... Explanations of the Old Testament and moral lessons are given by the Christian teachers". "Except in a few schools", Lerner confided to Montagu (March 1891), "the children have not learned to read or translate even a single line – yea, but one single word of the Bible! Can we expect these children to grow up into true Jews, capable of resisting the temptations of false doctrines and unbelief?"

It is clear that ideally the Committee would have preferred to have seen the *chedorim* phased out, and replaced by a more systematic scheme of instruction delivered in Board schools. However, realising that (on grounds of cost alone) such a reform could not be immediately realised, the Committee suggested instead that the *chedorim* be amalgamated and transferred, under the aegis of

Federation synagogues, into more suitable accommodation, perhaps in rooms made available in Board schools. An Education Committee was formed to encourage and monitor this process.

Progress was slow. On 29 February 1892, the Board of Delegates was informed that the *melamdim* (teachers) were showing "great reluctance to use rooms in the public schools for their classes, even when free, as they think this might endanger their means of livelihood". But in time some reforms were carried through. The *melamdim* were persuaded to agree to have their pupils examined in Hebrew and Religion "under the sanction of the Chief Rabbi ... in order to obtain certificates from him, as to their capabilities as teachers, and also that those who do not properly understand English will ... take lessons of any gentleman, appointed for their instruction". In the summer of 1894 the Federation agreed to send delegates to a conference convened by the JADRK "with reference to the religious education of Jewish children attending public elementary schools". Out of this conference was born the Jewish Religious Education Board (JREB), to which the Federation contributed by annual collections in its affiliated synagogues, and which endeavoured to provide more systematic and professional tuition for Jewish children attending schools in the public sector.

Lerner's efforts were not, therefore, without success. But he did not remain with the Federation long enough to witness the improvements which he urged. In 1892 he was drawn into a dispute, which was essentially domestic to the United Synagogue, concerning further proposed adulterations of the traditional form of worship. Chief Rabbi Hermann Adler invited him to a secret conference of United Synagogue Ministers, perhaps hoping that his presence would help defeat those who were pressing for liturgical reform, including the omission of certain prayers and the introduction of an English prayer in the Morning Service on Sabbaths and Festivals. On 12 July Lerner addressed a letter in the following terms to Samuel Montagu:

In connection with the Ritual question which is agitating all minds I beg to inform you that not without a sad and heavy heart the Chief Rabbi has yielded to the violent clamourings of some congregations for alterations in our prayers. But all who are faithful adherents of God and his doctrine will act entirely in harmony with his desires and feelings by holding fast to the existing order of prayer. We know from experience that all those who commenced with alterations of the Ritual of prayer have ended by shaking off the yoke of God's commandments and destroying all the foundations of Judaism.

London

Machzikep Hadass & shomre Shaboth

COMMUNITY.

The objects of the above community are, as indicated by its name, to uphold the Jewish Religion in this country, where, to our great regret, the foundations of our law have become weakened, and the whole structure of Religion is threatened, (as evidence the unsatisfactory state of provision of Kosher meat, Passover food and other requisites), and to prevent the Sabbath desecration which is much on the increase, there being seemingly, nobody able to put a stop to it. Some even favour the reform sects, who try to do away with the oral law altogether, retaining only such precepts of the written law which suit their personal inclinations, rejecting others, even principal laws of the Torah, which do not find favour with them—Who knoweth how much further this may lead to ?

And in order not to be mixed up with such people we have established this holy community in order that every one individually may be encouraged and strengthened by the union, to walk in the path of the law as revealed to us on Sinai and as explained by our teachers, the Rabbis of the Talmud and later authorities, the wells whose water we drink, viz. the Shulchan Aruch, and not to deviate from that path either to the right or to the left.

But to be sure to follow the right course we have to choose and elect a Rabbi great in wisdom and religious fervour

Shomrei Shabbos Society Rules, 1905

63

The reforms sanctioned by the Chief Rabbi did not of course affect Federation synagogues; on the contrary, the Board of Delegates warmly applauded Lerner's stand in defence of traditional Orthodoxy. But the experience appears to have led Lerner to reassess his own effectiveness in defending Orthodox Judaism in England. He founded a Shomrei Shabbos [Sabbath Observance] Society and, in the autumn of 1892, he and Montagu successfully intervened to prevent a non-Jewish employer dismissing a hundred Jewish tailors who would not work on the Festival of *Succoth* (Tabernacles). At the same time, however, Lerner began to investigate the possibilities of moving to another position. In late 1893 he applied for and was subsequently appointed to the post of Oberrabbiner of Altona and Schleswig-Holstein, a position which he took up on 1 June 1894.

Although the Federation was thus deprived of the services of its Minister, it had already acquired, in February 1894, those of a renowned *Maggid* (preacher), Chaim Zundel Maccoby (1858-1916), known as "The Kamenitzker Maggid" from the fact that he had earned for himself a lasting reputation as Maggid in the Russian town of Kamenitz-Litovsk, 1874-76. Maccoby was an early adherent of the *Chovevei Zion* ("Lovers of Zion") movement, formed in the Pale of Settlement in the 1880s as a non-political association to encourage Jewish settlement in Palestine, but without any thought or intention of recreating a Jewish state in the Holy Land – an enterprise which Maccoby regarded as heretical. Eventually (1883) Maccoby was appointed by the Chovovei Zion Association as its first full-time preacher. As a rabbi, Maccoby was certainly not in the first rank. His very considerable oratorical powers certainly drew large audiences, though they also made him many enemies. Some of these included rabbis who opposed the concept of *Chibath Zion* ("Love of Zion") and whom Maccoby, in turn, had no compunction in censuring for having failed to do anything to alleviate the miserable condition of Jews living under Tsarist rule. Unsurprisingly, Maccoby's sermons did not find favour in Tsarist circles. His lecturing activities were prohibited and in January 1890, with his wife and eight children, he fled to London, arriving in the same week in which Mayer Lerner was elected Minister of the Federation.

Maccoby came to London at an opportune moment. His fame had preceded him, and he was at once asked by Hermann Adler to deliver the *Hesped* (Memorial Address) for Adler's father, the late Chief Rabbi. Samuel Montagu was also much interested in him. Montagu had been one of the earliest adherents of the *Chovovei Zion* movement, an English branch of which Maccoby established on 4 April 1890. Maccoby moved easily within the milieux of the *chevrot*, earning money as a preacher and writing articles for the Jewish press. In 1892, Montagu suggested that the Federation appoint Maccoby as their Maggid, at a salary of £3 per week, which he, Montagu, would provide. Negotiations were not immediately successful, perhaps because Maccoby was

Chaim Zundel Maccoby c1900–c1915

not willing to give up his work for the *Chovovei Zion*. But in February 1894 he accepted the appointment (on the assurance that his other work could continue) at a salary of £150 per annum, the first £25 of which was to be "devoted to training that gentleman to preach in English". He remained Maggid of the Federation, at the same remuneration, until his death on 4 April 1916.

In his biographical essay on the Kamenitzker Maggid (in *Champions of Orthodoxy*, pp. 31-67), the late Julius Jung advanced the view that "a gentle rivalry" developed between Hermann Adler and Samuel Montagu, "each one anxious to win the Maggid for his own community". It is perfectly true that Maccoby accepted invitations to preach at the Great Synagogue, that he delivered the *Hesped* for Dayan Reinowitz, and that he joined Ministers of the United Synagogue in visiting Jewish patients in East End hospitals. After his naturalisation (July 1895) he became fiercely patriotic, and used his position in the pulpit to make appeals in aid of British soldiers wounded in the Boer War (1899-1902). The Chief Rabbi, who publicly supported British policy in South Africa at that time, must certainly have approved of these activities, although he espoused Conservative principles while Maccoby identified himself with Montagu's Liberal party.

Hermann Adler and Chaim Maccoby also agreed in denouncing Herzlian Zionism. Theodor Herzl, the Viennese journalist and self-confessed atheist, had published his proposal for a Jewish State (*Der Judenstaat*) in 1895. On 13 July 1896 Herzl was rapturously received in Whitechapel, where he delivered his first public address on the subject of political Zionism; a year later he summoned, at Basle, the first World Zionist Congress. The *Chovovei Zion* movement split. Maccoby regarded Herzl as a false messiah, and his movement as a threat to the preservation of Orthodox Jewish values. But it was Maccoby's influence that waned, not Herzl's. Hermann Adler voiced the authentic fears of the assimilated Anglo-Jewish gentry in denouncing the concept of Jewish nationality and the idea of Jewish statehood as "contrary to Jewish principles".

But he could not prevent the formation of the English Zionist Federation (January 1899) and he was as powerless as Maccoby to dissuade some very important Anglo-Jewish religious leaders, including Rabbi Werner of the Spitalfields Great Synagogue and Haham Dr Moses Gaster, the spiritual head of the Spanish & Portuguese Jews Congregation of London, from lending their patronage to the Herzlian Zionist movement.

Was it, perhaps, with an undertone of envy that the Kamenitzker Maggid condemned the views of a preacher – Herzl – whose sermons were at least as elegant and as compelling as his own? And was it, perhaps, an unwisely-directed stubbornness that compelled him to exploit the privilege of the pulpit by persisting in attacks on a view of the Zionist future which was widely held within Orthodox Jewry? Matters reached a head on 6 January 1900, when Maccoby was asked to attend a meeting of the Federation's Executive to explain his refusal to preach at the Vine Court Synagogue. His reasons were partly theological: the synagogue had been constructed with the *Almemar* (the platform from which services were conducted) immediately in front of the Ark. This arrangement, which smacked of the Reform movement, had the approval of the Chief Rabbi, though not that of Maimonides; a number of Orthodox synagogues in England were in fact built this way.

More plausibly, Maccoby confessed "that connected with the Vine Ct Synagogue there was a branch of the Zionist Society". Montagu, who chaired the meeting, was moved to point out that "the connection of branches of the Zionist societies with federated syn[ago]gues was no reason for the Rev. Mr. Maccoby's abstention from preaching in their pulpits". And (evidently with previous experiences in mind) it was, upon the motion of Hermann Landau, unanimously resolved to inform the Maggid that "in the case of any synagogue making a request to the Secretary in writing that the subject of Zionism should not be touched upon in sermons in their synagogues the Rev. Mr. Maccoby be asked to abstain from the subject accordingly".

This was not the first occasion upon which the Federation had had cause to censure Maccoby. In December 1897 the Board of Delegates had been obliged to consider complaints that he did not always pay the customary visits to members of the Burial Society observing Shiva. These complaints also touched upon the inordinate amount of time it was alleged he gave to "outside movements". Maccoby continued to attract large audiences. But though undoubtedly a great speaker he was not an outstanding scholar, and there was never any question of him succeeding Rabbi Lerner as Minister of the Federation. In spite of the identity of views between himself and the Chief Rabbi on a number of subjects, he was never at ease in the anglicised Jewish circles in which Hermann Adler moved so easily.

Gradually Maccoby distanced himself from both Hermann Adler and Samuel Montagu, offering his strict vegetarianism as the pretext for refusing social invitations. In 1910 his health began to deteriorate. He was gradually released from his duties and was retired, on full salary, just two months before his death, at the comparatively early age of 58. In agreeing – as we must – with Julius Jung's view hat "Rabbi Maccoby died exactly as he had lived, in poverty and distress", we must also point out that though some of the blame must be laid at the door of the Federation (which did not increase his salary once during his period of service), his own intense pride prevented him from accepting, from Samuel Montagu and Lord Rothschild, honoraria which others would justifiably have accepted without demur.

Early in 1895 an approach was made to Dr Moritz Grunwald, the Chief Rabbi of Bulgaria, to succeed to the vacancy created by Mayer Lerner's departure. In March Grunwald, then 42 years of age, travelled to London to preach in Federation synagogues, but died with great suddenness during his visit, and was buried in the Edmonton cemetery. The matter of a replacement for Lerner remained in abeyance for several years. We may only speculate as to the reasons why. The controversy between the Chief Rabbi and the Machzike Hadass community was then at full flood, and Samuel Montagu may have felt unwilling to add to Hermann Adler's worries by consenting to the appointment as Federation Minister of an eminent rabbi who would in all probability have outclassed him as a Talmudic scholar. Then again, the number of foreign rabbis who could have filled the position, and who were fluent in English as well as in Yiddish, was small.

At all events the Federation had not sufficient money of its own to engage a Minister, and Montagu did not raise the matter formally until the meeting of the Board of Delegates held on 9 July 1901 – the same meeting at which the decision was taken to admit the Spitalfields Great Synagogue. At that meeting Montagu announced that he would provide the sum of £1,000 to cover the salary of a Minister for three years. The candidate chosen for the post, by methods more diplomatic and discreet than those which had accompanied Mayer Lerner's election was Moshe Avigdor Chaikin (1852-1928). Rabbi Chaikin had been born in Russia (to parents who were adherents of the Lubavitch Chassidic movement) and possessed Rabbinical Diplomas from some of the most eminent East European rabbis, including the saintly Yitzhak Elchanan Spector of Kovno. But at the time of his "call" to the Federation he was Minister in Sheffield, having been appointed there in 1892 on Hermann Landau's personal recommendation.

The appointment of Chaikin was not only different in kind from that of Lerner – in that the former was not elected at all, but given the post of Federation Minister on the authority of Samuel Montagu, who merely informed the Federation (18 October 1901) of what he intended to do – but coincided with, and may have been the outcome of, a broadening of the horizons of the Federation, perhaps reflecting in turn an evolution in Montagu's thinking about the future activities of the organisation he had created.

By the beginning of the twentieth century the Federation was playing a very central part in the daily lives of East End Jewry. It was represented, even if inadequately, on the major Anglo-Jewish communal institutions.

In connection with the Board of Guardians, the Federation had been instrumental (1891) in establishing a nursing system for the sick Jewish poor. It had promoted evening classes to enable Jewish immigrants to learn English. It was, as we have seen, taking steps to reform and improve Jewish religious education. The *chedorim* were gradually replaced by better-organised and regularly-inspected Talmud Torah classes conducted in connection with and often on premises provided by Federation synagogues. In 1895 the Talmud Torah Trust was launched (with a gift from Montagu of £1,000), in order to make grants to Talmud Torahs and supervise their work. The Federation was also vigorous in upholding the legal right of Jewish parents to withdraw their children from non-Jewish religious instruction in Board schools; in 1895 it had persuaded the London School Board to take urgent action to ensure that this right was not infringed.

Moreover the Federation was, by virtue of its activities and its status, achieving some of the objects which Montagu had had in mind for it. It patently did not entice Jews away from socialism, but its existence probably did something to blunt the anti-religious edge of socialist propaganda. As they became naturalised and enfranchised, the immigrants and their children gravitated naturally towards a left-wing view of politics. Yet, at the same time, socialists and trade-unionists learnt to respect religious values even if they did not agree with them (which was by no means always the case). More importantly, the Federation was bringing order and organisation to bear upon the activities of the *chevrot*, but in a way that preserved the self-respect of the immigrants. Montagu was the Federation's patron, yet the Federation did not behave in a patronising manner towards its affiliated congregations. The cramped, steamy *chevrot* were replaced by small, intimate synagogues, many built directly or indirectly with Samuel Montagu's money; but the daily management of these buildings remained in the hands of those who worshipped in them.

In 1894, on the recommendation of the Liberal Prime Minister, Lord Rosebery (the widower of Hannah Rothschild, Lord Rothschild's cousin) , Montagu had been made a baronet, and six years later, at the age of 68, he retired from the House of Commons, to be succeeded in the Whitechapel seat by his nephew, Stuart Samuel. Already recognised as an expert on the immigrant question, Montagu now turned his attention to finding ways in which Jews might be encouraged to leave the overcrowded East End and settle not just in the suburbs of London but in other cities, where their presence in relatively small numbers would - it was hoped – not attract such adverse comment from the host community. A spontaneous movement out of the East End ghetto had already begun, but those immigrants who moved away naturally retained their links with the Federation, while others looked to it to provide the sort of facilities (such as access to a burial ground) which they were not yet in a position to afford themselves. Montagu was keen to encourage the dispersion of Jews from inner London, and saw the Federation as a valuable tool to assist in this process.

On 20 October 1901 the Board of Delegates had placed before it an application for affiliation from the Reading Hebrew Congregation. The Board resolved "that the principle of affiliating Orthodox provincial congregations is hereby approved, and that it be referred to the Executive Committee to prepare promptly a scheme for carrying this resolution into effect". In due course the Reading Congregation became a Federation affiliate, and on 6 November Montagu, hoping to capitalize on this success, addressed to provincial congregations a circular letter inviting them also to form closer links with the Federation and suggesting an annual conference at which matters such as immigration, migration and naturalisation (but not religious questions, which Montagu deemed to include Zionism) could be discussed. Although Montagu used the word "affiliate", it is evident that he did not intend provincial communities to have as close a relationship with the Federation as London congregations: on payment of a minimum of £5 annually, they were to be allowed representation at the Board of Delegates, but not voting rights. However, they were to be encouraged to use the good offices of the Federation in any secular or religious matter, and the Maggid or Minister of the Federation was to visit them at least once a year.

Responses to this letter were varied. Only twenty congregations declared themselves in favour of the principle of "affiliation"; others showed no enthusiasm for the idea, but did favour a conference to discuss common problems. Thus in May 1902, under the auspices of the Federation, the first-ever conference of Jewish communities of the British Isles took place, attended by 93 delegates representing 43 different congregations. It was as a direct result of a resolution passed at that gathering, expressing the opinion "that the disadvantages caused by the overcrowding of Jews in our large towns ought to be alleviated by a distribution from those centres to other places where work is obtainable under more salubrious surroundings", that the Jewish Dispersion Committee was established, by Montagu, the following year. The Committee offered employment and financial help to those Jews wishing to move out of London; in this way some (though not many) Jewish families were sent to Reading, Leicester, Blackburn, Dover and (perhaps) Stroud in Gloucestershire.

However, since there was little enthusiasm among provincial communities for formal "affiliation", the Federation took some initiatives of its own in the London suburbs. In June 1903, it called a public meeting "for the purpose of encouraging and stimulating removals from the congested areas [i.e. the East End] to Tottenham and surrounding districts". The Tottenham Hebrew Congregation was in due course established, being admitted into the Federation on 1 February 1904. Help was also extended to Jewish families living in Canning Town. Hermann Landau advanced a loan of £200 to the Walthamstow synagogue (March 1903), and the movement of Jews to localities in the vicinity of Enfield was stimulated by the affiliation (January 1907) of the Tottenham Hale Congregation. In a significant passage in its Biennial Report for 1903-04, the Federation gave notice that it would no longer assist "in the establishment of new synagogues in the congested area in East London, believing that ample synagogal accommodation is now provided (save for the exceptional requirements of New Year and the Day of Atonement) for existing needs".

It is clear that Montagu not only foresaw the movement of Jews away from the East End, where his Federation had been founded. He actively encouraged this movement, believing that the Federation had a vital part to play in the lives of the 'second generation.' It is equally clear that he envisaged an enhanced role for the Minister of the Federation in this emerging situation. Avigdor Chaikin's activities were not to be restricted to the East End. In Sheffield he had had charge of two congregations; in the service of the Federation he would act as a knot, binding together fifty or more communities that had affiliated themselves to an organisation of national importance in Anglo-Jewry. Hermann Adler's approval of the appointment, and his attendance (as well as that of Haham Gaster) at Chaikin's installation at the New Synagogue on 15 December 1901, was therefore of some importance to Montagu, for if the Minister of the Federation was to be welcomed in the provinces, the imprimatur of the Chief Rabbi would be of decided advantage.

Hermann Adler's attitude towards the Anglo-Jewish clergy was at this time undergoing some modification. Recognising at last that his refusal either to award *Semichot* (Rabbinical Diplomas) or to recognise those awarded by others was leading to a grass-roots repudiation of his authority, he conferred Diplomas upon two 'Englishmen' (both Russian-born but educated in London and graduates of Jews' College), the Reverends Asher Feldman and Moses Hyamson. Early in 1902, following the death of Dayan Spiers, these two newly-appointed rabbis were elevated to the Beth Din. Federation Jews, who had hoped that at least one east European rabbi would be appointed, were deeply upset. The facts were that Lord Rothschild had refused to countenance such an appointment, and that the United Synagogue had made it clear that one of the principal tasks of the new Dayanim would be to assist in the

Anglicisation of the Jewish East End. On 1 March a well-attended meeting held in the large hall of the Aldgate Baths, Goulston Street, protested against

Those who mean to appoint for us East End Jews as Rabbis, persons whom we by no means recognise as such, by the word Rabbis we understand well known and highly educated men in Talmudic learning.

Rothschild was unyielding. But Hermann Adler seems either to have been sympathetic to the complaints or to have feared that a genuine repudiation of the Beth Din's authority would ensue on a scale far greater than that involved in the *Machzike Hadass* schism. Adler consulted the Honorary Officers of the United Synagogue and, within a week or so, invited Rabbi Chaikin to participate in the work of the Beth Din, without, however, being assured of a permanent place on it and, indeed, without the title of Dayan.

This arrangement, though obviously far from ideal, appears to have caused immediate satisfaction to all concerned. Hermann Adler had salvaged his reputation. The authority of the Beth Din was assured. The prestige of the Federation had been enhanced. And no additional financial burden fell upon the United Synagogue. But over the course of time, as Chaikin was prevailed upon to undertake an ever greater share in the Beth Din's work, rumblings of dissatisfaction with his anomalous status began to be heard from the Federation side. In its Biennial Report for 1903-04 the Federation pointed out that Chaikin was "devoting the major portion of his time and attention to the general communal needs rather than to those of the Federation", and that he was "to all intents and purposes" carrying out the duties of a Dayan: "he is in daily attendance for dealing with Shaaloths [Questions] and sits regularly at the Beth Din".

The feeling grew that Chaikin should either be elevated to the full status of a Dayan, or be withdrawn from the Beth Din to devote all his energies to the Federation. Early in 1906 the ailing Dayan Susman Cohen announced his retirement. It was hoped – apparently on the basis of a gentlemen's agreement – that Chaikin would replace him. But the Honorary Officers of the United Synagogue offered a string of excuses for their refusal to assent to this proposal. The Board of Delegates of the Federation lost patience and, fully supported by Montagu, announced in July 1906 that Chaikin had been requested "to once more devote his entire time to the services of the Federation and to cease acting as Dayan".

Avigdor Chaikin did eventually become a Dayan of the Beth Din, but not within the lifetime of Samuel Montagu. The affair seems to have soured irrevocably Montagu's relationship with the United Synagogue, and it led him to reassess his former policy that the Minister of the Federation should function only under the authority of the Chief Rabbi. In 1907 Montagu was elevated to the peerage as Lord Swaythling. On 24 July he addressed to the Federation a letter in which he announced his intention, "in commemoration of the honour conferred upon me … to select a Chief Minister of the Federation. He must have a great reputation for Orthodoxy, must be a Doctor of Theology & a good Orator, also a gentleman of refined manners, about 40 years of age & able to take a prominent position among Jewish clerics. He will co-operate in all Orthodox movements acceptable to our Board".

What was meant by the term "Chief Minister", and how would that post differ from the one to which Chaikin had been appointed six years previously? Montagu explained – to some extent – what he had in mind when he addressed the Board of Delegates on 28 July 1907. His speech is important both for its substantive content and for its implied criticism of Chaikin's shortcomings as Federation Minister:

> it was desirable to have some centralised efforts by a gentleman of great attainments … They wanted a gentleman with a great deal of vigour, who would attract crowds to hear him preach, and who would be so great a scholar that no-one could or would dispute his authority; he must, in addition, devote his whole time to the welfare of working class Jews … what

was wanted was a man who would be a friend to the people, a man full of energy, attraction and ability. The Chief Minister of the Federation would co-operate with the existing authorities, with the Chief Rabbi and with the Spanish and Portuguese Synagogue.

Montagu seems to have desired a person who would combine the oratory of Chaim Maccoby, the Maggid, with the Talmudical scholarship of the Minister, Avigdor Chaikin, but who would also have a sound training in the values of western European civilisation and who would therefore be capable of making an impact as a social worker helping, in particular, to combat the twin attractions of materialism and "Liberal" Judaism. But in the carefully chosen words "Chief Minister", and in the absence, now, of any reference to the sanction and authority of the United Synagogue's Chief Rabbi, might we not be justified in supposing that Montagu had in mind an appointment parallel and not subordinate to that of the Chief Rabbi, and that he was therefore opening up the possibility that the Federation might have to strike out on its own, as a *kehilla* (organised community) totally independent of any other?

In his speech Montagu also referred, enigmatically, to an unnamed person whom he was considering for the post of Chief Minister. But he was destined not to make the appointment. In 1908 he became seriously ill and, though he partially recovered the following year, the matter of the Chief Minister was not, during his lifetime, brought to a successful conclusion. His last attendance at the Board of Delegates was made on 8 November 1910. His death came on 12 January 1911, just a few months before that of Chief Rabbi Hermann Adler, whose faltering authority he had, in truth, done so much to bolster.

Samuel Montagu lived and died an exceedingly wealthy man: the gross probate value of his estate was valued at no less than £1,150,000 (equivalent to about £100 millions at 2017 values).The day of his funeral – he was of course buried at the Edmonton cemetery - was one of great general and heartfelt mourning in London's East End. Even in death he remained the ever-generous benefactor of the Federation he had created. In his will Montagu bequeathed £2,000 for the continued payment of salaries to rabbis Chaikin and Maccoby, and he also, in a breathtaking but entirely characteristic act of charity, left to the Federation all moneys owing to him in respect of loans made to various affiliated synagogues.

CHAPTER THREE

A Change of Direction

In retrospect it is clear that the decision of the Federation's Executive Committee (28 February 1911) to elect Louis Montagu as the Federation's second President was a mistake. But at the time the decision seemed entirely natural, and was taken as a formality. Born in 1869, Louis Montagu was the eldest son of Samuel, and therefore heir to the Swaythling title. This fact alone marked him out for the presidency, a succession that his father had specifically requested. The increasingly independent posture of the Federation, more especially in relation to the United Synagogue, demanded that, if possible, the office of President be given to a peer of the realm – the equal (so to speak) of the head of the House of Rothschild. Significantly, Louis Montagu became at once "President", not "Acting President" as his father had been. No doubt, too, the Executive Committee hoped that the Federation would continue to benefit from the munificence of the Swaythlings by keeping the presidency within the Montagu family: the new Lord Swaythling became President and at the same time the post of Treasurer, which he had vacated, devolved upon his younger brother, Gerald.

But Louis Montagu was not the man that his father had been, and did not share his father's religious outlook. It is a remarkable fact that the staunch piety of Samuel Montagu seems to have repelled rather than to have attracted his children. Two of his daughters, Marian and Lilian, were founders of Liberal Judaism, "the objects of which [he declared in his will] I strongly disapprove". His second son, Edwin, was to enjoy a political career more distinguished than his had been, for he rose to become Secretary of State for India in David Lloyd George's coalition government during the First World War. Edwin – regarded in some quarters as a future Liberal leader, was a champion of Indian self-rule. He was also an inveterate opponent of Zionism, and it was partly through his efforts that the draft Balfour Declaration was altered in several important respects so as to make it less favourable to the Zionist viewpoint.

Edwin's anti-Zionism was shared by his eldest brother. Like many of his generation of Anglo-Jewish leaders, Louis regarded Herzl's Zionist movement as a profound danger to the safety and standing of the Anglo-Jewish community. Samuel Montagu had been one of the very few leading British Jews to have given Herzl a warm reception. "He confessed to me," Herzl recorded in his diary (24 November 1895), "– in confidence – that he felt himself to be more an Israelite than an Englishman." But in this regard, as in so many others, Samuel Montagu had been very much the exception to the rule and, in any case, he was in due course alienated by Herzl's lack of personal respect for Jewish Orthodox values. Most of the Anglo-Jewish leadership was repelled by the very idea of Jewish nationality: they regarded being Jewish simply as a connotation of a set of religious beliefs. The possibility of Jewish nationhood struck at the heart of the process of social, cultural and political assimilation of which they were so proud. Without a Jewish state they were well-bred British Jews – Britons of the Jewish persuasion. With it (so the argument went) they automatically became exiles in the land of their birth, and their loyalty to Great Britain could be questioned. The battle for Jewish emancipation had been fought and won on the grounds that an English Jew was different from an English Christian only by virtue of his religion: admit the Zionist claim (so the argument also went) and you admitted too that the Gentiles had been deceived at the time (1858-60) emancipation had been granted – just a few years before Louis Montagu himself had been born.

At the time of his elevation to the presidency of the Federation these views did not attract a great deal of adverse comment. We noted in the previous chapter how sensitive the Federation had been to Rabbi Maccoby's objections to political Zionism. On the other hand, before 1914 the English Zionist Federation was still a small body, with plenty of supporters amongst the immigrants but without power or influence at the centre of the community, let alone at the parliamentary or governmental level. Palestine was under the control of the Turks. The achievement of the Zionist aspiration seemed nothing more than a dream, and, therefore, the philosophical disputations between Zionists and anti-Zionists appeared as no more than a minor irritant. Events during the Great War, the conquest of Palestine by the British army, and the promulgation of the Balfour Declaration (2 November 1917) were to inject into these disputations an air of stark and intense reality. But in 1911 these developments could not be foretold.

Quite apart from his anti-Zionism, however, Louis Montagu was on other grounds quite unsuited to the post of President and to the time at which he had been elevated to that office. In 1911, with almost a quarter-century of experience behind it, the Federation was a major communal organisation, in which the principle of self-rule was strongly entrenched, and which rightly regarded itself as the foremost bastion of an Orthodoxy which was under attack. In February 1905, for example, it had taken the grave step of severing its links with the Jewish Religious Education Board, following the failure of the JREB to take action against one of its vice-presidents, Claude Montefiore, who (the Federation's report for 1905-06 declared) had publicly attacked "the genuineness of the Decalogue" and had rejected "the authority and authenticity of the Mosaic Law". The resolution implementing this withdrawal was couched in uncompromising terms:

That the Federation being an Orthodox body cannot contribute towards a Jewish Education Board who have elected for one of their leaders a gentleman who has openly denied the Fundamental Principles of Judaism.

Fortified with a gift of £1,000 from Samuel Montagu, the Federation immediately established a Trust to finance the teaching given in Talmud Torahs, "On which the vitality of Orthodox Judaism so greatly depends".

The rift with the JREB lasted for six years. In 1911 the Federation returned to the Board, but on its terms. Louis Montagu ought to have learned from this dispute, which related not merely to the Federation's Orthodoxy but also to its growing impatience with lack of proper representation on major communal bodies. But these lessons appear to have been lost on him. In his 1937 history of the Federation, Dr Cecil Roth recorded that Louis Montagu "was possessed of a particularly strong sense of duty, but he lacked his father's generosity, his devotion and above all, his deep feeling of interest and sympathy with the Orthodox East End masses". Louis Montagu had hitherto taken little interest in the Federation, and he assumed the presidency of it almost as a sinecure, chairing its meetings and signing its correspondence but increasingly leaving its day-to-day affairs in the hands of Joseph Blank, the Secretary, who (in Roth's words) began "to treat it almost as his private preserve". This, too, was to store up trouble for the future.

Almost immediately upon taking office, Louis Montagu was confronted with two interconnected problems: the appointment of a Chief Minister, as his father had wished; and the choice of a successor to Chief Rabbi Hermann Adler, whose death in July 1911 triggered a new crisis in the ongoing uneasy relationship between the Federation and the United Synagogue. We need not take too literally the verbose resolution passed at a special meeting of the Federation's Board of Delegates called to announce Adler's demise. On a personal and family level there was sympathy, of course. But there was no disguising the fact that Adler had been unloved in the East End, and that his death had provided – from the Federation's point of view – an opportunity to press the claims of the immigrants in securing as Chief Rabbi a man whose Orthodoxy they, the bulk of Anglo-Jewry, might freely respect. Should these claims not be met, the Federation could proceed to elect its own Chief Minister, a move which some saw as a precursor of total schism.

Both Samuel Montagu and Lord Rothschild had clearly been aware of this danger, and of the strength of the forces urging the Federation to go its own way. In June 1910, the Honorary Officers of the Federation, together with the Secretary, had met their counterparts of the United Synagogue, at New Court (the Rothschild headquarters), to discuss whether it might be possible (in Samuel Montagu's words) "to prevent friction in the election of an eventual Chief Rabbi, when our respected Chief, who is over 70, is not able to work any longer at his post." (Newman, pp. 95-96). Montagu offered a formal merger with the United Synagogue, but on terms which Rothschild rejected because Federation representatives on the United Synagogue Council would have formed a majority. Montagu also offered the United Synagogue a say in the appointment of the Federation's "First" (presumably Chief) Minister, who would be "Delegate Chief Rabbi and eventually Chief Rabbi". This offer, too, was refused.

With Hermann Adler's death the question of Federation participation in the election of the Chief Rabbi could no longer be avoided. The stance adopted by the United Synagogue was that the apportionment of votes at the conference to elect Adler's successor should be based on the financial contributions made to the upkeep of the Chief Rabbinate by the participating congregations. The Federation took a more democratic stance. In one of the many letters that passed between them on this subject, Joseph Blank wrote to the United Synagogue Secretary, Philip Ornstein, thus:

If the Federation of Synagogues is to be properly represented on the body dealing with the election of the Chief Rabbi, it must not be in proportion to its contribution to the Chief Rabbi's Fund ... but to the immense interest it represents in the religious life of the community. It necessarily follows, then, that the elective influence must be in proper ratio to the membership, which numbers 6,500 in the 51 Synagogues represented. [23 November 1911]

In January 1912, a more strident tone was set, in a letter signed not simply by Blank himself but by Louis Montagu, Hermann Landau (Vice-President) and the two Treasurers, Gerald Montagu and Mark Moses. "Under any well-conceived and logical method of representation [they pleaded] all members of Jewish congregations in the United Kingdom would have such a share in the election as their numbers justified." But the leaders of the United Synagogue stood firm in their resolve that financial considerations alone should prevail: the Federation was offered 28 votes, while the Honorary Officers of the United Synagogue were to have no less than 75 at their disposal, not counting those votes case by constituent congregations of the United Synagogue, which would thereby command about 340 votes in all. On 30 May 2012 Blank gave the Federation's definitive response:

> *The Board cannot give its adhesion to a scheme which practically secures to the United Synagogue, representing as it does only about one-sixteenth of the Jews of the United Kingdom, the election or dismissal of the Chief Rabbi.*

So it was that the election as Chief Rabbi of Dr Joseph H. Hertz (16 February 1913) took place without the participation of the Federation, which shortly afterwards, and following an acrimonious correspondence between Blank and Ornstein, declared that it would refuse any longer to contribute to the Chief Rabbi's Fund.

The dispute over the Chief Rabbinate was certainly bitter, but it was not sterile. From it the Federation and its members derived several advantages. Although the United Synagogue was determined that wealth should prevail over numbers, Lord Rothschild and his colleagues did recognise that the apparatus of the Chief Rabbinate and the Beth Din had to be made more attractive to East End Jews. Shortly after Hermann Adler's death one of the Vice-Presidents of the United Synagogue, Albert H. Jessel, proposed to Louis Montagu that Rabbi Chaikin be permitted to rejoin the Beth Din as a full Dayan, a position to which the Council of the United Synagogue subsequently appointed him (at a salary of £100 per annum), and with which the Board of the Federation (6 December 1911) enthusiastically agreed.

Chaikin's elevation to the Beth Din was universally popular amongst Federation members, even though it meant that he had less time to devote to purely Federation interests. A modest, peace-loving man, Chaikin laboured at the Beth Din for no less than fifteen years, enhancing its status and providing, incidentally, one of the few formal links then existing between the Federation and the United Synagogue. He continued to worship at the Old Castle Street synagogue, where he gave frequent sermons in Yiddish and a daily lesson in Talmud. But after the death of his wife (1923) he determined to settle in Palestine, where his only daughter lived, and in August 1926 he resigned his position in England to join his family in the Holy Land. There, in Tel Aviv, he died on 17 June 1928.

When Avigdor Chaikin joined the United Synagogue's Beth Din, and once it became clear that the Federation was not to be allowed to participate fully and fairly in the election of a Chief Rabbi, the appointment of its own Chief Minister acquired a new urgency. Advertisements were placed in the English and foreign press, and Hermann Landau, Mark Moses and Joseph Blank travelled to the Continent to meet and interview between twenty and thirty applicants. The choice, made by Louis Montagu under the terms of his father's trust deed, fell upon Dr Meir Zvi Jung, the rabbi of Ungarisch Brod in Moravia, then part of Austria-Hungary.

Meir Jung was destined to spend only nine years in the service of the Federation, but his impact was truly worthy of a lifetime's endeavours.

Born in Hungary *circa* 1858, he had studied at many of the leading *yeshivot* of central Europe, but had also attended the universities of Marburg and Heidelberg and had received a doctorate from the University of Leipzig for a thesis on the *Pirkei Avoth* (Ethics of the Fathers). In 1886 he accepted a rabbinical position in Mannheim, Germany, and was married in the same year to Ernestine Silberman; six children were born of this union, of whom one, Julius (1894-1975), was also to play a central part in the development of the Federation of Synagogues. In Mannheim Rabbi Jung acquired a reputation as an indefatigable and outspoken opponent of Reform Judaism. In 1891 he accepted a call to Ungarisch Brod. There, in his search for ways of combating anti-Orthodox and assimilationist tendencies, he pioneered the establishment of Jewish day schools, which offered instruction in both religious and secular subjects. That at Ungarisch Brod opened in 1901. Another, in Krakow (Poland), commenced in September 1906 but was closed down a month later after hysterical opposition from an unprincipled alliance of assimilationists and Chassidim; but other schools flourished at Lemberg (Lviv, Galicia), Storozynetz (Bukovina) and Vienna.

On his arrival in London (28 May 1912) Jung explained to the *Jewish Chronicle* why he had accepted the post of Chief Minister of the Federation: "If I had craved a life of ease, I could have stopped in Brod, but the wider scene and scope presented in London proved too attractive to me. I am a worker and I already know that in London there is much work to do." He expanded on this theme in the address which he gave at his installation (16 June 1912), an impressive ceremony which took place at the Philpot Street Great Synagogue – the first time that a Minister of the Federation had been installed in one of its own affiliated synagogues. Stressing the importance of the study of Torah, he declared that "the Torah must not be adapted to the age, but the Torah cannot ignore the age", and he dedicated himself to work with the young in order to realise the values of Judaism without retreating from the secular world. "If the spirit of the age does not forcibly impose itself on the Torah, Judaism must be carried into that spirit and brought into harmony with the spirit of the

Torah ...This conception of Judaism can best be carried into effect through the Federation, containing as it does within its ranks considerable talent, that will always labour for the honour of Judaism".

In the nine years of life that remained to him, Meir Jung made a remarkable impact upon the Federation and upon Anglo-Jewry. In part, this impact derived from his unquestionable Orthodoxy, in respect of which the members of the *Machzike Hadass* community paid him a singular tribute. The death of Rabbi Werner, on 20 December 1912, left the Spitalfields Great Synagogue without a spiritual leader. On 14 January 1913 the Federation received a letter from the Spitalfields Great asking whether, pending the appointment of a successor, Rabbi Jung might attend the Synagogue to answer *sha'alot* and, in short, act as its religious mentor. This request was of course granted. Until 1915, therefore, Jung provided in his person a link between the Federation and the *Machzike Hadass* and became, in the years immediately prior to the Great War, the acknowledged champion of Orthodox Jewish observance in London.

Philpot Great Street Synagogue, 1922

The task of maintaining and strengthening this observance in the face of mounting economic and social pressures occupied a place of priority in Jung's work. To assist in this task he founded the *Va-ad HaRabbonim* (Council of Rabbis) of the Federation of Synagogues, of which he became President and Rabbi Avraham Yitzhak Kook (Rav of the *Machzike Hadass* 1916-19) Honorary President. Other leading members of the *Va-ad* included rabbis S. I. Bloch, T. H. Ferber, P. Gerber, M. Zimmerman, A. Schonfeld and M. T. Schwartz. The *Va-ad* provided a forum for rabbinical debate and policy formulation on matters such as the regulation of Kashrut, the supply of *Mikvaot* (ritual baths), the standard of teaching at Talmud Torahs, and more general questions of religious education. More subtly, it acted as a pressure group to enhance the status of the rabbinate, especially in relation to local and national lay leaderships.

Believing that the key to the maintenance of Orthodox values lay in the education of the youth, Jung felt that the establishment of Jewish day schools, where secular studies might be combined with religious instruction, was as necessary in England as in central Europe. But a rapid survey of the situation in east London led him to a further conclusion: that in order to persuade poverty-stricken parents to keep their boys (not girls) at school, it would be necessary to make some sort of payment – otherwise the boys would surely be sent out to work at the earliest opportunity.

Thus was born the idea of a Jewish Trade School, where practical instruction in a vocational trade was to be combined with religious instruction, and wages were to be paid. Louis Montagu, Hermann Landau and the banker Otto Schiff lent their support to this venture. In December 1912 the first Jewish Trade School was opened, at which boys received seven hours technical instruction each weekday; religious instruction was in the hands of Rabbi I. Kyansky, the headmaster of the Great Garden Street Talmud Torah, and wages were paid to the boys at a minimum rate of seven shillings and six pence per week. Initially, twenty boys received instruction in the tailoring trade. Later, when the roll increased, instruction was also provided in the manufacture of leather trunks. As the venture expanded, larger premises were found at Cambridge Heath (Bethnal Green).

The School was brilliant in conception. Had it succeeded, many of the problems experienced by later generations of British Jews – particularly in relation to the lack of Sabbath observance and of religious knowledge generally - might have been considerably lessened. In fact, the School failed, not through any fault of Jung but because the sums of money needed to keep it going were not forthcoming. An appeal for £500 fell on deaf ears. This may have been because the School was not perceived as an urgent necessity. It is more probable, however, that the underlying strict Orthodox values of the School did not find favour with the lay leaders of Anglo-Jewry, and that it was not regarded (unlike the Jews' Free School) as an instrument of assimilation. The School was therefore allowed to die.

Rabbi Jung then turned his mind to other ways of strengthening Orthodoxy, particularly in the matter of Sabbath observance. He initiated discussions with Jewish trade unions, both in London and the provinces, in order to bring home to their members the importance of Sabbath observance in the face of low wages and unemployment; on 14 December 1919, in Manchester, the unions convened a conference to discuss these issues. Jung also addressed the problem of supporting and stimulating Orthodoxy among the younger, post-school generations, amongst whom the drift away from Jewish values was already alarmingly apparent. To stem the tide he established a network of Sinai Associations, first in London and later in major provincial centres. These associations were affiliated to the Sinai League, and comprised junior and senior branches; they combined social and literary activities with Jewish study and, in practice, had a strong Zionist inclination. In London most of the Sinai branches met at Federation synagogues, and Federation personalities were prominent in the League's activities.

Jung was also responsible for a number of other initiatives in the field of Jewish Orthodoxy. In July 1914 he was instrumental in establishing, in the East End, a branch of the non-Zionist Agudas Israel movement, dedicated to the strengthening of Jewish unity through adherence to the Torah. During the First World War the East End movement languished, but was later revived, Jung becoming secretary of its London branch (1920-21). Believing that future generations of rabbis needed to be able to relate more sympathetically to the modern world, he took steps to have secular studies introduced into the curriculum of the famous *Etz Chaim* ["Tree of Life"] yeshivah, then located in Hutchinson Street, off Petticoat Lane. He also established a *Tomchei Torah* ["Supporters of the Torah"] Society, for the benefit of elderly Jewish scholars, and he established a network of "Sabbath Observance Halls" to provide a range of suitable activities for the enjoyment of the Sabbath.

It is evident that the deliberate manner in which Rabbi Jung acted in the pursuit of Orthodoxy was greeted with mixed feelings in Federation circles. By the truly Orthodox his efforts could not but be applauded, as indeed they deserved to be. One wonders, however, just how deep was the impact of his work upon a generation of English-born Jews, eager to escape from the poverty of the East End and seeing in Zionism and socialism the ideal tools for this job. In any case, upward social mobility, in which the children and grandchildren of the immigrants naturally participated, was already pushing Jews out of the East End and into the suburbs of north, north-east and north-west London. In these areas the United Synagogue was ready with the resources necessary to finance synagogue-building. Jung does not seem to have evinced much interest in these developments.

Neither did Louis Montagu. Afraid that Jung's popularity among the Orthodox (symbolised in his special relationship with the *Machzike Hadass* community) might lead to a new schism in Anglo-Jewry, Montagu offered Jung's services to the United Synagogue's Beth Din as an additional Dayan, whose entire salary would continue to be paid by the Federation. This offer was refused (December 1913), perhaps as a result of new quarrels that had broken out over kashrut and other matters.

The continued sale of forbidden fat (*chelev*) in hindquarters meat had led to demands that the Chief Rabbi should prohibit the sale of hindquarters altogether. There were doubts, too, about the *matzot* baked under the supervision of the Beth Din, and about the *mikvaot* maintained under its auspices. It must be said at once that, whatever Louis Montagu's personal prejudices might have been, he pressed upon the United Synagogue, with vigour and without compromise, the views of Federation members. In a statement to the Board of the Federation he declared that

> The Executive of the Federation intended to see that the Community in the metropolis, even the Community in England, did not glide from Orthodoxy to laxity, because of the weaknesses of those institutions controlling the religious matters of the Community. He considered it the duty of the Federation, the duty of his late father to do his best to prevent such a calamity ... Unless the United Synagogue satisfied the religious scruples of the Orthodox in a reasonable time, the Federation, at no matter what sacrifice, would have to find ways and means of assisting those who desired the Laws of their fathers carried out in the spirit and in the letter.

Negotiations with Chief Rabbi Hertz proved fruitless, since any proposal to give the Federation parity of status with the United Synagogue was naturally vetoed by the latter's lay leadership. In March 1920 Jung, on behalf of the *Va'ad HaRabbonim*, wrote to the Honorary Officers of the United Synagogue offering the services of the *Va'ad* in supervising shechita. In reply (28 April 1920) the United Synagogue's deputy secretary advised Jung that if he wished to prefer "charges" against any butcher operating "under the authority and supervision of the Chief Rabbi and Beth Din, who constitute the supreme Jewish Ecclesiastical Authorities in this country", he should take his complaint to the Board of Shechita. The status of the Federation's *Va'ad* was never acknowledged, and the United Synagogue deemed its own dignity more important than the maintenance of kashrut – the proper preparation and sale of kosher food.

Jung died on 10 June 1921. The *Jewish Chronicle* wrote of him:

Rabbi Jung ... fully conceived as his duty the necessity for doing all that lay in his power to strengthen the traditional conception of Judaism among the members of the Federation of Synagogues ... To this purpose he devoted himself with unswerving loyalty ... He was cast in the uncompromising mould which would allow nothing to circumstances and condition, if they impinged upon the rigid adherence to the letter of the Law ... there is always something admirable in the rock which, fixed among shifting sands, weathers all storms ... In these days, when compromise is raised to the level of a virtue and do as you please and go as you like are the fashion ... men of the calibre of Rabbi Jung are sorely needed.

The efforts which Jung and others made for the sake of kashrut were, however, eventually crowned with success. As a result of persistent pressure by the Federation and by Rabbi Dr Victor Schonfeld's *Adass Yisroel* Synagogue, the Slaughter of Animals Act (1933) replaced the Chief Rabbi as the sole authority to licence *shochtim* (slaughterers) by a Rabbinical Commission of ten rabbis, of whom only four were nominated by the United Synagogue while two were nominated by the Federation, one by the Union of Orthodox Hebrew Congregations and two by the President of the Board of Deputies to represent provincial congregations. With this welcome breach in the absolute prerogative of the United Synagogue's Chief Rabbi, the prohibition of the sale of forbidden hindquarters meat swiftly followed. In October 1934, following negotiations with Rabbi Yechezkel Abramsky of the *Machzike Hadass*, the Chief Rabbi prohibited the selling of hindquarters meat unporged; in June 1935 Abramsky became a Dayan of the Beth Din.

By this date Louis Montagu was no longer in charge of the affairs of the Federation, which had undergone an internal revolution. To understand why, and with what significance, we must return to the years of the Great War and immediately thereafter. Although Dr Hertz acted, perforce, as the spokesman of the lay leadership of the United Synagogue – at least in religious matters – his appointment had marked a watershed. In choosing him to succeed Hermann Adler, Lord Rothschild had borne in mind the necessity to appoint a man as acceptable to East End as to West End Jews. The election of Hertz fulfilled this condition, more particularly as it brought to the office a man of strong Zionist convictions as well as of considerable religious scholarship. The anti-Zionist establishment could thus no longer turn to the Chief Rabbi for support and, in denying this establishment the legitimacy it craved, this establishment clung, therefore, to its hold over the two leading secular organisations in the community, the Anglo-Jewish Association and the Board of Deputies of British Jews. The former was a purely self-elected body, upon which the immigrants were not represented at all. The constitution of the latter – the Deputies – did not allow for the representation of the many friendly societies and small synagogues to which the immigrants belonged and which they had created.

In the years immediately preceding the Great War one can detect, both within and beyond the Federation, a growing impatience on the part of the immigrants and their children with the continued dominance of Anglo-Jewry by the old ruling families. Louis Montagu's handling of the dispute over the Chief Rabbinate had attracted criticism from some sections of the Federation because of his failure to consult sufficiently widely among the membership at large. Yet the dispute itself, and more especially the support that the Federation received from provincial communities, ought to have acted as a warning to those members of the ruling elites who supposed that they could continue to act in the twentieth century as they had done in the nineteenth, without reference to the feelings of those who destinies they controlled. Much more sensitivity was called for. But in his approach to Zionist matters, Louis

Montagu conducted himself in a totally insensitive and quite reprehensible manner.

In late 1916 a British army occupied the Sinai Peninsula, and the following March the British invasion of Palestine began. Led by the Manchester chemist Dr Chaim Weizmann, British Zionists worked feverishly to extract from Lloyd George's government some promise to allow the re-establishment of a Jewish national entity in the Holy Land. The Anglo-Jewish gentry took fright. A manifesto against the Zionist movement was prepared, and it appeared, in *The Times* of 24 May 1917, in the form of a letter over the signatures of D. L. Alexander (President of the Board of Deputies) and C. G. Montefiore (President of the Anglo-Jewish Association). This letter purported to represent the views of Anglo-Jewry. Yet its contents – indeed its very existence – had been kept a closely-guarded secret. Repudiations of the letter quickly appeared from Lord Rothschild, Dr Weizmann and Chief Rabbi Hertz. Alexander was forced to resign after a stormy meeting of the Board of Deputies, whose constitution was subsequently (1919), altered so as to broaden considerably its representative base. The Federation was henceforth entitled to six delegates, quite apart from those elected by individual Federation-affiliated synagogues; in 1919 some twenty Federation synagogues were represented at the Board of Deputies in this way.

The ousting of D. L. Alexander from the presidency of the Deputies amounted to a revolution. In the words of the *Jewish Chronicle* (22 June 1917) it was "a revolt against a system of oligarchic repression", and in fact had less to do with Zionist sentiment *per se* than with a feeling – widespread within Anglo-Jewry – that the old ruling cliques had had their day. The members of the Federation were, however, deeply sensitive to attacks upon the Zionist movement. Louis Montagu's open identification with the anti-Zionists gave rise to much disquiet. He had supported the infamous letter to *The Times*. On 25 June 1917 some members of the Federation's Board of Delegates called upon the Federation to issue a public disapproval of that letter, and the following September there was a further attempt to publicly distance the Federation from the views of its President. At a meeting of the Executive Committee (20 November 1917) Montagu ruled that "the Federation as such was precluded from a discussion on political questions", and called the bluff of his detractors by offering to resign. The offer was not taken up.

However, although forced to admit that in supporting the anti-Zionist manifesto he had acted in a purely private capacity, Montagu did not heed these early-warning signs. He proceeded to take a leading part in the discussions which led, a week after the promulgation of the Balfour Declaration (2 November 1917), to the establishment of the League of British Jews, the objects of which were "To uphold the status of British subjects professing the Jewish religion", "To resist the allegation that Jews constitute a separate Political Nationality", and "To facilitate the settlement in Palestine of such Jews as may desire to make Palestine their home". At the League's first General Meeting (14 March 1918) Lionel de Rothschild was elected President and Louis Montagu Vice-President.

These activities, too, attracted much bitter comment from within the Federation. At a special meeting of the Board of Delegates, held at 17 Leman Street on 14 January 1918 and attended by 100 delegates, a vote of No Confidence in the President, moved by V. Shapiro of the Philpot Street Great Synagogue and seconded by L. Quint, of Montagu Road, attracted 26 votes, but 44 voted against it. So Louis Montagu survived once more, but only by a small majority (representing 18% of those present). Although 30 delegates had abstained, they certainly could not be considered Montagu supporters, and the fact was that less than half those present had indicated their approval of Montagu's conduct.

In spite of the wealth and social status of its members the League of British Jews never amounted to much; Louis Montagu's position in it might still have been forgiven. But in April 1919 he committed another and much more serious indiscretion. The High Tory *Morning Post* had published a series of article entitled "The Causes of the World Unrest", in which Russian Jews living in Britain were branded as emissaries of Bolshevism. While the Board of Deputies and the English Zionist Federation did their best to dispel groundless fears, ten leading members of the League, including Montagu, wrote to the *Morning Post* (23 April 1919) a mischievously-worded letter: in the course of dissociating themselves from any revolutionary sympathies, they implied that such sympathies were indeed held by significant numbers of their co-religionists, and they accused the *Jewish Chronicle*, and its sister paper the *Jewish World*, of promoting the Bolshevik cause.

An examination of the precise motives of those who wrote this letter forms no part of the history of the Federation. What is relevant is that its publication, in a newspaper which was openly and unashamedly anti-Semitic, clearly marked a turning-point in the deteriorating relationship between the Federation and its second President. The wonder is that this relationship endured for a further six years and more, and the explanation for that probably lies in the esteem in which the Swaythling family was held by older generations of Federation members. It is in this connection surely significant that the early 1920s saw the deaths of many leading members of the Federation associated with the endeavours of its founder. In particular, Mark Moses, who had served with Gerald Montagu as Treasurer, died on 22 May 1921. Rabbi Jung died on 10 June, and Hermann Landau passed away on 25 August.

It is also noteworthy that by this time the Federation had outgrown entirely its reliance upon the charity of the Swaythling family – though it must also be said that this new-found financial independence itself owed a great deal to Samuel Montagu's financial largesse. As synagogues repaid to the Federation capital that Samuel Montagu had advanced, the Federation was able to increase the sums available as loans to other synagogues in need, either to refurbish or to rebuild their existing premises. But the major cause of the Federation's new-found affluence was its Burial Society. In the financial year 1912-13 the Society had 5134 subscribers in 55 synagogues; the weekly subscription of two pence brought in £1,922, but the cost of funerals amounted to only £1,854. With assets of £5,500, and freehold land ample for the needs of the next twenty-five years, the Burial Society was able to offer a "first class" funeral to all subscribers, and to increase the *shiva* benefit from 20 shillings to 30 shillings. Moreover, it was able to make a grant of £100 to the Federation in 1912, and to double that grant in 1913. By 1915 the size of the grant had reached £500, part of which was devoted to the Talmud Torah Trust; at the same time members of the Society on active service during the Great War were exempted entirely from their obligation to pay contributions "until their safe return".

A special Actuarial Valuation of the Burial Society carried out in the autumn of 1920 showed its membership to be no less than 9,484, an increase of 72% on the 1914 figure. On the one hand this very substantial increase obliged the Society to begin searching for a second cemetery, and to help build up funds for this purpose the weekly subscription was raised to three pence as from 1 April 1921. On the other hand, the Society's income, more especially from those not in membership of Federation synagogues, permitted it to change in a fundamental way the manner in which it contributed to the general funds of the Federation. As from 1 April 1920 the Burial Society made over to the Federation one penny per week for every subscriber. In 1921 this produced no less than £1,646. The Federation of Synagogues now had its own guaranteed regular income: it had become entirely self-supporting.

And so began the final act in the drama of Louis Montagu's presidency of the Federation. To administer its new-found wealth, the Board of Delegates (21 May 1921) appointed a Finance Committee, whose members were drawn from a generation that did not feel towards the second Lord Swaythling any of the deference shown to the first. They were in fact deeply suspicious of Louis Montagu, and they and their friends became increasingly restive at the autocratic manner in which the Secretary, Joseph Blank, conducted the Federation's affairs.

The character of Joseph Blank remains an enigma. We know that he was born in Whitechapel in 1866 and that he was educated at the Jews' Free School. We do not know how he occupied himself between leaving that school and becoming the first Secretary of the Federation, just a few months after his 21st birthday. From the minute-books and correspondence of the Federation he emerges as an aloof, almost pompous figure, whose English ways must certainly have seemed strange to Federation members with whom he was in daily contact. By the turn of the century he had himself moved away from the East End, to a house at 119 Farleigh Road, Stoke Newington – the address from which the Federation itself operated until, in 1925, it took possession of permanent offices at 64 Leman Street (Whitechapel), the headquarters of its Burial Society.

Blank – in the words of Cecil Roth – had come "to rule the Federation with an iron hand". He was able (more especially during and immediately after the Great War) to summon meetings infrequently and to conduct the affairs of the Federation in a highly personal manner. For example, in 1920 the Board of Delegates met only twice, and the Executive Committee but once! These meetings, in any case, did little more than endorse the decisions of the Honorary Officers, which decisions had in turn been prompted by the Secretary.

The establishment of a Finance Committee, on the recommendation of the Executive, had the effect (almost certainly intentional) of opening up this closed system of government, which had rested basically upon the prestige of Louis Montagu and the confidence he reposed in Joseph Blank. When apparently well-founded suspicions were voiced concerning Blank's stewardship of the finances of the Federation and its Burial Society, and when Blank departed for Monte Carlo, demands for his dismissal grew ever louder. But Montagu defended him. The criticisms of Blank turned, therefore, into a call for the ousting of the existing Honorary Officers. We know, from the reports in the Yiddish newspaper *Die Tsait*, that in or by January 1925 what was termed a "Vigilance Committee" had been formed, and that by this date it had set itself the task of securing an end to the Swaythling administration. A meeting of the Board of Delegates (13 May 1925), at which no less than 172 delegates were present, dismissed the Secretary but expressed its desire that Montagu should continue in office for the time being. At another Board meeting, on 25 November, Montagu and the then Vice-President, Councillor Harry Kosky (elected June 1923), were actually re-elected to office. But their insistence that Blank be awarded a substantial pension was ignored. They resigned their offices and, in a statement, made it clear that their decision was irrevocable.

These events were important in themselves, of course. The departure of Louis Montagu marked the end of an epoch in the Federation's history. His death, on 11 June 1927 (at the age of 57) was not universally mourned in the East End, as his father's passing had been, and the bitterness over what were regarded as serious betrayals of trust remained for many years afterwards. Beyond these considerations, however, we are surely justified in seeing, in the passionate controversies that attended the final years of his presidency, a deeper sociological significance. Many of those who attacked Joseph Blank could be found defending Louis Montagu, hoping that he would remain their President: for them, the prestige and the memory of the Swaythling family were still very important. Others, however, clearly used the alleged misdeeds of the Secretary to attack the person of the President. This attack was justified partly on the basis of Montagu's public conduct since 1917, as we have seen; but it also smacked of class antagonism.

It is during the stormy meetings of 1925 that we first encounter Councillor Morris Harold Davis. An East Ender by birth (1894), Morry Davis had joined the Stepney Borough Council in 1920, and had enjoyed a truly meteoric rise within the ranks of the Stepney Labour Party, combining as he did the qualities of rhetoric, political cunning, charm and ruthlessness. Davis represented a new breed of East End Jew, one foot planted in traditional Judaism, the other in the Zionism and socialist egalitarianism that had already begun to take hold of the Jewish East End. His elevation to the presidency of the Federation symbolized the victory of the immigrant classes over the Anglo-Jewish gentry that had sought to control them and manage their affairs – at least as far as the Federation was concerned: the triumph of a popular local figure (who became Mayor of Stepney in 1930) over a moneyed aristocrat.

At the Board meeting of 13 May 1925 it was Morry Davis who had voiced the mood of no confidence in Louis Montagu's leadership, and who had had the courage to give public utterance to the suspicions concerning Joseph Blank. It was he – Davis – who obtained the largest number of votes (53) in the election of a three-man sub-committee charged with the duty of finding a new Secretary. And at the fateful Board meeting of 25 November 1925, the last which Louis Montagu attended, it was Davis who had moved and carried a portentous resolution: "That despite any rule or minute to the contrary, that at any meeting of the Federation, where any delegate desires to address the meeting in Yiddish, such permission be granted". Montagu's lame reply, that "he could not understand Yiddish, and therefore could not be responsible for the conduct of proceedings in a language he was unacquainted with", must surely have sealed his fate, for his plea that the dispensation as to Yiddish should not come into effect until the election of a new President was simply ignored.

At that meeting Davis was elected both as a Treasurer of the Burial Society (together with J. M. Libgott), and as a member of the Finance Committee; in addition, he was appointed a Federation representative to the Board of Shechita and the Board of Deputies. His continued refusal to countenance any pension for Joseph Blank met with widespread support. At a Board of Delegates meeting held on 2 December 1925 Davis was (according to the Minutes) "received with acclamation" and his confession that "he had joined the Federation in order to fight Lord Swaythling on his infamous letter to the Morning Post" was warmly received. In January 1926 Davis was elected an

Honorary Officer of the Federation. That same month he and his supporters forced through the Burial Society a motion to make donations totalling £150 to Zionist causes (the *Keren Hayesod* and the *Keren Kayemet*). The Federation thus became, to the delight of Zionist fundraisers, the first significant non-Zionist organisation in Anglo-Jewry to contribute to the redemption of the National Homeland. In February similar resolutions were approved by the Board of Delegates, and grants of increasing magnitude were made to the *Keren Hayesod* and the *Keren Kayemet* (Jewish National Fund) regularly thereafter.

At a meeting of the Board of Delegates held on 17 November 1926, over which Libgott (who had chaired Federation meetings since Louis Montagu's resignation) was unable to preside owing to an indisposition, Davis was voted into the chair. And at a Delegates' meeting on 20 March 1928, with an attendance of over 200, Davis was elected both Treasurer of the Burial Society and President of the Federation of Synagogues – but only by 79 votes to 51: fewer than half those attending chose to support him. It is pertinent to ask why, and why his succession to the presidency took so long. That some Federation members hoped to entice back Louis Montagu is not in doubt; but by June 1926 it had become certain that any such hope must be abandoned. Others felt that some person of eminence unconnected with the recent tumults might be induced to accept the presidential office – and it is clear that approaches were made, but without success. Davis was a young man of undoubted talents, a forceful speaker (in both Yiddish and English), a passionate champion of Zionism, in short a natural leader of East End Jewry. But it is also evident that there were those within the Federation who feared his ambition, and who were perturbed that so much power (the combination of the offices of Burial Society Treasurer and Federation President) should be concentrated in one man.

For the moment, however, these fears appeared quite groundless. One reason for this was that the rise of Morry Davis to the presidency coincided with the appointment of a new Secretary, Julius Jung, who took up office in

November 1925. By training an analytical chemist, Jung had had to abandon this career owing to the difficulties of Sabbath observance, and instead entered Jewish communal service, becoming Secretary of the Sinai League founded by his father. In the course of his long association with the Federation (1925-59), first as Secretary and later as Executive Director, Jung was able to combine a love of Torah-true Judaism with a sound business mind: integrity, efficiency and compassion were the hallmarks of his work, and his many talents were later recognised by the Board of Deputies, of whose Aliens Committee he became Chairman. Through his efforts, and those of his colleagues, many hundreds of refugees from Nazism were brought to safety in the United Kingdom, and it was equally due to him, in substantial measure, that the Federation itself was able to survive the upheavals of the Second World War.

Jung took over the secretaryship of the Federation at a time of multiple crises, but also of optimism and growth. In 1926 Federation synagogues had on their books 12,565 families, representing something in excess of 50,000 souls; by 1937 the number of families had increased to about 13,000, and the number of affiliated synagogues (51 in 1912) had grown to 68. During the inter-war period, therefore, the Federation was indeed the largest synagogal body in the United Kingdom: male membership of the United Synagogue in 1930 totalled only 8,310. Under Councillor Davis and Julius Jung the Federation responded to the central position it now occupied in the affairs of Anglo-Jewry, and played a leading if controversial part in the life of the community.

The major aims of the new administration were, in due course, embodied in a revision, in 1934, of the "objects" of the Federation, which henceforth included the following:

I.   To grant loans, free of interest, & on such terms as the General Council of the Federation may from time to time decide, to affiliated Synagogues for the purpose of erection, reconstruction or redecoration of their House of Worship …

II. To assist in the maintenance of Orthodox religious instruction in Talmud Torahs and Yeshivoth.

III. To obtain and maintain Kashruth by direct representation on the Board of Shechita or by such other means as the Board may from time to time decide.

IV. To support by grants and/or by representation on other councils other worthy Jewish and non-Jewish charities here and abroad.

V. To promote by other means the interests of Synagogues affiliated to the Federation.

VI. To use influence and exertion (other than political) whenever intervention may seem desirable, in favour of Jewish Communities throughout the World.

VII. To further the upbuilding of Eretz Yisroel and thereby create a haven of rest for our brethren who are persecuted because of their race and religion in many countries.

The mention, in the first of these objects, of the "General Council", referred to a revision of the constitutional machinery of the Federation which was carried out at the same time. The General Council consisted of the presidents of the affiliated synagogues, and other members, elected by the synagogues every three years, in the ratio of one member plus one member for each complete number of fifty members, with a maximum of 12 per synagogue: each member was to be a male of at least 21 years of age, in membership of the Burial Society. The General Council elected an Executive Committee of 16, of which, in addition, the President, Vice-President and the two Treasurers of the Burial Society were *ex-officio* members; the quorum for meetings of the

Executive was seven. Moreover, the Federation President, or in his absence the Vice-President, or in their absence either of the two Treasurers, was to "have power to take action in case of emergency when it may be impracticable to convene the General Council or the Executive Committee".

Wiser counsels might have prevailed, to block the adoption of a constitution which did in theory make possible the rule of an oligarchy, or even of one person. Voices were indeed raised against the hasty implementation of the new scheme. But in 1934 Davis carried all before him, pleading – correctly – that the income-tax authorities required the adoption of new rules before they could consider the question of charitable status. This status was soon granted, and a tax refund of over £900 obtained, a success which the General Council (24 September 1935) greeted with a round of applause!

Although, therefore, the adoption of the new constitution amounted to an excessive concentration of power, for the time being good results were clearly forthcoming. One such was the abolition of interest on advances made by the Federation to affiliated congregations. The originator of this reform was a Mr B. Simons, of the Bethnal Green Synagogue, who at the Board of Delegates on 28 February 1927 moved:

> That this Board of the Federation resolves, in accordance with the laws of our Bible, to charge no more interest on the loans advanced to the Federation of Synagogues and that in future the policy of the Board be to grant loans to the Federated Synagogues free of interest.

Replying to the debate on this proposition, Davis observed that "the profit the Federation will make will be in Yiddishkeit". The motion was carried by a large majority.

Davis was also instrumental in enhancing the prestige and status of the Federation both within and beyond Anglo-Jewry. In spite of its greatly increased membership the representation of the Federation upon the Board of Shechita was still only half that of the United Synagogue; nor was any

Federation delegate numbered among the members of the Board of Shechita's Executive Committee. There was, in addition, very strong criticism of the criteria used by the Shechita Board in distributing moneys to charitable causes – in particular (according to the debate at the Federation's Board of Delegates, 12 August 1928), its "disinclination to help Talmud Torahs". There was some talk of the Federation establishing its own shechita authority. In the event, and after negotiation, Federation representation upon the Shechita Board was doubled (from five to ten delegates), and in July 1931 Davis became one of the Shechita Board's Vice-Presidents.

At the same time the Federation signalled its disapproval of the management and functioning of the Talmud Torah Trust by withdrawing from it. The Federation's Board of Delegates was told on 29 October 1928 that the Trust

London Jewish Hospital, 1930

had become "nothing but a distributing centre of money given to them by the Federation and the Jewish Religious Education Board ... Inspection of Talmud Torahs was inadequate, many teachers were not capable of teaching nor were they keeping Traditional Judaism". The Federation and its affiliated synagogues determined that henceforth their Talmud Torahs would receive their funding directly from the Federation, acting on the advice of an Education Committee elected by the Board of Delegates and charged with the duty of maintaining "the teaching of Judaism in accordance with the Orthodox traditions". Grants to the Trust were only resumed in 1930, when the Trust was reconstituted and the Federation allotted seven out of the ten places on its Executive.

We should also note that in August 1929 the Federation obtained representation upon the management of the *Etz Chaim* yeshiva, in return for which a grant was given to the yeshiva of £250; by 1930 the level of this grant had more than doubled. Other Jewish institutions that benefited from the financial prosperity of the Federation in the inter-war years included the London Jewish Hospital, the Home for Aged Jews, the Jews' Temporary Shelter, the B'nai B'rith First Lodge of England, the Jewish Lad's Brigade, Jews' College, the Beth Jacob schools in eastern Europe, some eighteen yeshivot in Poland, and the British Fund for Polish Jewry (to which the Federation made a grant of £10,000 in 1936). On 24 April 1932, following a visit from Dr Hertz (the first time a Chief Rabbi had ever addressed the Federation), a grant of £1,000 was made to the Bayswater Jewish Schools. Annual grants were also continued to the Board of Guardians and the Visitation and Welfare Committees for London Jewry, and the Federation undertook to bear the entire cost of a Superintendent for the mikvaot in the capital.

Some smaller grants are worthy of particular note since they reflect the broad outlook of the Federation under Councillor Davis's guidance. In 1930 the Federation undertook to contribute half the salary of a Yiddish interpreter at the Whitechapel County Court. The following year a grant of

£25 (subsequently an annual grant) was made to the University of London's School of Oriental Studies in support of lectures on the Talmud. In 1934 a grant of £105 was made to the Lord Mayor's appeal for funds to help victims of the Gresford Colliery disaster (north Wales), in which 266 miners had lost their lives. Another act of charity towards coal-miners had already taken place (significantly, perhaps, it was not mentioned in Cecil Roth's history of the Federation published in 1937): in 1929, in response to a personal appeal by Davis, eight Federation synagogues, ignoring political sensitivities, donated small sums, totalling with interest just over £18, to relieve economic distress among mining communities.

During the Davis era two developments stand out as indicating the radical stance of the Federation within both British Jewry and the wider Jewish world.

The Federation identified itself totally with the Zionist effort. Not only were very substantial grants made to the Jewish National Fund (plus a loan of £10,000, in 1933) to assist in the work of rebuilding the Jewish National Home; considerable sums of money were also donated to a variety of other Zionist causes, such as the Hebrew University of Jerusalem and the Balfour Forest. Following the massacre of Jews by Islamic terrorists in Hebron (1929), the Federation established a special Palestine Emergency Fund. Moreover, the Federation was not afraid to enter the political arena in defence of Jewish national interests. A series of resolutions condemning the policy of the British administration in Palestine was forwarded to the Prime Minister, J. R. MacDonald, on 12 September 1929. On 9 January 1936, at Davis's prompting, the General Council resolved to deplore the proposed establishment in Palestine of a Legislative Council on which Jews would have been outnumbered by Arabs by a ratio of two to one.

Events in Palestine took place against the grim backcloth of the rise of Nazism in Germany. In this regard the Federation, under Davis's leadership, placed itself firmly on the radical wing of the Anglo-Jewish community. As early as 22 May 1933 the Board of Delegates had passed and communicated to the British government and the League of Nations a resolution condemning persecution of Jews in Germany and calling for the easier passage of Jews to Palestine and to the UK. Between 1933 and 1935 the Federation contributed no less than £17,000 to the Central British Fund for German Jewry. The Board of Deputies sought to avoid confrontation with the British government over official attitudes to the Third Reich. But the Federation played a leading part in the formation of the Jewish Representative Council for the Boycott of German Goods and Services, which was launched in November 1933. Unlike the Board, the Federation did not distance itself from the World Jewish Congress. And in 1943 the Federation was active in urging the election of Deputies who would support the re-establishment of the Jewish State, thus helping to ensure that there would be no repetition of what had happened at the Board in 1917.

The presidency of Morry Davis was therefore marked by a much deeper and more outspoken involvement by the Federation in matters that touched upon the Jewish world. In consequence the Federation was looked upon as an Anglo-Jewish institution of the first importance. We have already noted the visit of the Chief Rabbi. During the 1930s other notables who called upon the Federation to enlist its aid included the former *Haham* of the Spanish & Portuguese Jews, Dr Moses Gaster, Dr Nahum Goldman of the World Jewish Congress, and Dr Chaim Weizmann. We have also briefly noted the Federation's continued expansion during this period; the precise nature of this growth now requires more detailed consideration.

In his 1937 history Dr Roth observed that the Federation was "now no longer a predominantly East End organisation". This was perhaps an exaggeration, but the thought that prompted it – that affiliated congregations were then to be found in all parts of London – was certainly true. Two processes were working simultaneously to produce this result. Federation members who moved away from the East End were not easily enticed into the United Synagogue, and were often disposed to establish new places of worship which might function within the framework of independence that affiliation to the Federation allowed. On 12 August 1928 two congregations were admitted which exemplified this outlook, the Clapton Synagogue and the Stamford Hill Beth Hamedrash; the latter rapidly acquired a reputation as a bastion of Orthodox learning, where classes and study-circles flourished under the guidance of Rabbi Dr. E. W. Kirzner; the former commenced life in a ramshackle house in Lea Bridge Road, but moved within a few years into an imposing edifice purpose-built on the same site. Other congregations admitted into the Federation in the inter-war period included Central Hackney (July 1927); Walthamstow (October 1928); Fulham & Kensington (September 1929); Gladstone Park & Neasden and Leytonstone (both April 1932); Willesden (December 1933); Bermondsey (March 1935); Forest Gate (July 1937); and Springfield, Upper Clapton (January 1938).

By the time of the outbreak of the Second World War the Federation could therefore boast congregations from Stamford Hill and Tottenham in north London to Bermondsey and Woolwich in the south, and from Shepherds Bush and Notting Hill in the west to Forest Gate in the outlying eastern suburbs. As a result of its greatly increased membership the Federation Burial Society took under urgent consideration the purchase of a new burial ground. In 1936 a

Rainham Cemetery, 2017

site of some 106 acres was acquired at Rainham, Essex, and was consecrated on 20 February 1938 by Dayan Dr A. Feldman, Rabbi Dr Kirzner and Rabbi A. Singer.

The cradle of the Federation remained in the East End, but there too we may observe signs of change. As Jews moved out of the East End, many of the older and smaller synagogues ran into financial difficulties. In presenting the Balance Sheet to the Board of Delegates on 22 May 1933 one of the Treasurers, I. M. Shockett, referred "to Synagogues who had made no repayment [of loan] during the year under review & warned them that a test case will have to be made in order to emphasise the sanctity of agreements". This warning was repeated before the General Council on 14 March 1935, when Davis named two congregations, Cannon Street Road and Commercial Road Talmud Torah, as having "made no repayments for some time", and Shockett named a further two (Chevrah Torah and Artillery Lane) which "apart from not paying back the money advanced to them had not even had the courtesy to reply to two letters sent to them by the auditors". In April 1936 the General Council applied a sanction to synagogues which did not repay loans on time: the rebate of one-eighth of the Federation contributions collected by them would no longer apply.

At the General Council of 30 June 1938 we hear, for the first time at such a meeting, talk of the necessity of amalgamating smaller synagogues. Some amalgamations had already taken place: of the founding congregations of 1887, only three were numbered among the 69 affiliated synagogues a half-century later. But a major hindrance to the process of rationalisation and amalgamation was that the Federation itself could do no other than encourage and exhort. The synagogues were part of the Federation, but were not 'owned' by it. Legal control of these synagogues was vested in particular trustees; in some cases these gentlemen had died or could not be traced.

In December 1936, by 52 votes to 44, the Federation approved constitutional changes which meant that any synagogue applying to be admitted to the

Federation, or any Federation-affiliated synagogue applying for a loan, would henceforth be obliged to agree that at least one of its trustees should be appointed by the General Council. This amounted to a subtle change in the federal relationship, and the narrowness of the majority (in spite of Morry Davis's personal backing for the proposals) is itself a reflection of their contentious nature. In fact the new arrangements had little immediate impact, for they were not retrospective. The arrangements were basically sound and long overdue; had they been implemented much earlier in the Federation's history, many of the post-1945 difficulties that the Federation experienced would in all probability have been considerably lessened.

Prayer Hall at Rainham Cemetery (2018)

CHAPTER FOUR

A Time of Stress

Under the presidency of Morry Davis the Federation of Synagogues came to exert considerable influence within Anglo-Jewry. Much of the credit must go to the President himself, who possessed a comprehensive knowledge of the community (beyond as well as within the metropolis) and who spared no effort to make the Federation's voice heard in national as well as purely communal arenas. As a leading East End socialist he had unashamed political ambitions, which might have led to a seat in Parliament. There were those who accused him of using his position in the Federation as a launching pad for his political career, and there may be some truth in this allegation. Yet it must also be recorded that Davis had plenty of friends and admirers within the Federation; without them, he could never have held office for so long, less still could he have manipulated it in a way that eventually became a communal scandal.

Davis's extraordinary tenure of the presidency cannot be fully understood except in the context of his hegemony of the Stepney Labour Party. His position in the Federation helped him to the mayoralty, and his chairmanship of certain key committees of the Stepney Borough Council made his friendship worth cultivating by those – very many of whom were of course Jewish – who lived in the borough. In the 1920s and early 1930s the Labour Party in Stepney was engaged in a fierce struggle to gain control of the Council, in which – following the local elections of November 1931 – the balance of power was held by a group of independents led by the well-known Jewish communal worker Miriam Moses, chairwoman of the St. George's Liberal Association. As the foremost Jewish communal leader in the borough Davis was an obvious asset to the Labour Party in its efforts to win these independent seats.

In 1934 Labour did so: it won every seat on the Council. By means of a long-standing alliance with local Irish Labour leaders, Morry Davis tightened his grip on the local party machine. However, he seems to have played very little active part in combating the Fascist menace in Stepney in 1936, and in February 1937, together with three other Jewish councillors, he voted to allow the British Union of Fascists to hold a meeting in Limehouse Town Hall. During the tense atmosphere of 1936 one of the most remarkable champions of Jewish rights locally was the then Mayor, Councillor Helena Roberts, by birth a Jewess but by conversion a Christian. In proportion as Roberts sought to obtain a more even-handed approach by the police, so Davis (still the Labour Leader of the Council) seems to have taken umbrage against her – to the extent, in July 1938, of using a procedural device to prevent her proposing a committee of inquiry into allegations of police brutality against anti-Fascists.

Why did Davis adopt these postures? The most likely explanation is that he needed to do so in order to placate those whose support was necessary for his long retention of the Council leadership. By the late 1930s certain aspects of this leadership had become highly controversial. This aspect of Davis's career is beyond the scope of the present work. Yet it is surely no coincidence that we first encounter criticism of Davis as President and in the records of the Federation of Synagogues in the summer of 1938, by which time his reputation as a defender of Jewish interests was clearly becoming seriously tarnished. In the Federation, as in the Stepney Labour Party, the coalition of interests that had promoted him in the later 1920s was, a decade later, beginning to fall apart.

As we noted in the previous chapter, Davis had been raised to the presidency in 1928, when a new Board of Delegates had been elected. No further election of Delegates or Council members was ever held during the entire sixteen years of his tenure of office. At first the omission to hold elections seems to have been passed over in silence – a sign less of adulation than of apathy. Later, the excuse was cheekily offered that the holding of new elections would interfere with the promulgation of the revised constitution. Later still, Davis explained that it was only right and proper that those who had been responsible for the purchase of the Rainham cemetery should be in office when it was consecrated.

By then (1938) Davis was able to use his powers under the new constitution with a cynical disregard of the most fundamental tenets of democratic practice. But – again it must be stressed – he did so with the acquiescence and even approval of the overwhelming majority of synagogue grandees. Mild criticism of the failure to hold proper elections was indeed voiced at a General Council on 30 June 1938, but was easily brushed aside. In 1939 the criticism became more intense: one Council member likened Davis's conduct to "Hitler business", while another (Jack Goldberg) "begged him to fix a date for the General [Council] election".

The formation of an organized opposition to the regime, and the holding of "unofficial meetings" (as Davis termed them) was a signal for the more public defence of what had, by then, become a dictatorship. Davis announced that elections for a new General Council would be held during 1939. What is more, he summoned a meeting of the Presidents of Federation synagogues to hear him reaffirm this pledge (14 May 1939). Significantly, however, he refused to send out any formal notification to this effect. Julius Jung's manuscript note of this meeting is worth quoting:

> *The Presidents, who had attended in very large numbers, were asked to express their views on the matter, and it was remarkable with what unanimity they expressed themselves as fully satisfied with the statement that the President had made. President after President rose to express his Synagogue's pride in the management of the Federation, on the splendid work that is being done on behalf of World Jewry.*

Davis and his supporters cleverly turned the meeting into a show-trial of the "Constitutional Group", whose members were accused of putting their own interests above that of the Federation, and of giving ammunition to its enemies, amongst which the *Jewish Chronicle* (which had carried reports of the opposition to the Davis regime) was accorded a place of high priority. As befits a show-trial, one delegate was persuaded to make a public recantation, as Jung recorded:

> *Mr. Mann (Cannon Str[eet] Rd) made a confession. He stated that he was the instigator of the unofficial meetings because he had thought that there were no reasons for postponing the election. Had he attended more regularly, he might have known better. He promised, after having heard the President's statement, to leave the opposition who have misled him and to support Mr. Davis wholeheartedly.*

Before the gathering dispersed, Davis gave a brief résumé of his presidency, comparing it with "the old management", to the inevitable detriment of the latter. "The Presidents [Jung recorded] listened with obvious satisfaction to this imposing statement of facts, already partly forgotten by them and left the meeting satisfied that a mischievous bubble had been safely burst and that the Federation is doing work of which they could justly continue to be proud."

Davis's promise, made at that meeting in May 1939, that elections (but only for Honorary Officers and Executive members) would be held "this year" was – unsurprisingly – never kept. The opposition to his rule found a new champion in Dr Bernard Homa, a grandson of Rabbi Werner and himself a leading member of the *Machzike Hadass* synagogue. Homa and his friends were able to insist upon a meeting of the General Council, held on 13 June and attended by some 209 delegates. In a powerful speech he declared that "the constitution of the Federation ... had been violated. Notices of Motion ... had never appeared on the Agenda; two requisitions [for a General Council] have been ignored ... There is too much intimidation abroad". Furthermore, Homa "protested against the non-attendance of the Hon. Officers to a summons from the Beth Din". But at the end of a heated and at times angry debate the Constitutional Group was defeated by 99 votes to 78.

Later in the year, and again with the support of the synagogue presidents, Davis used the excuse of war to postpone even the elections for Honorary Officers and the Executive. On 10 November 1940 a meeting of the General Council was asked by him to agree to the following resolution, which was passed *nem con*:

> *That, in view of the present state of emergency, the General Council hereby resolves that, unless otherwise determined by the General Council or until one month after His Majesty the King shall have declared that the present state of emergency no longer exists, whichever shall be the earlier, the Executive, acting by a majority of those of them able to be present at a meeting, be and are hereby appointed to exercise in their absolute discretion on its behalf all powers and discretions at present residing in or conferred upon it by the Rules and Bye-Laws of the Federation.*

The following month a meeting of presidents with the Executive agreed "that all vacancies on the Executive be filled by the Executive", because (it was alleged) of "the inadvisability of calling delegates' meetings at the present moment". In the immediate context of the war and the Battle of Britain, these extraordinary steps might have been justified for a very limited period. In fact, although the General Council met several times subsequently during the war (for example on 9 May 1943 to discuss the forthcoming triennial elections to the Board of Deputies, which the Zionists were determined to 'pack' to prevent a repetition of what had happened in 1917, and again on 9 September 1943, when no less than 171 delegates assembled to discuss a dispute with the United Synagogue over claims for war damage to synagogues), it was never permitted to discuss new elections. Davis used the excuse of war to extinguish totally the representative nature of the Federation of Synagogues, and to turn it into an instrument of his own will.

Suddenly, in the latter part of 1944, the Davis era came to an abrupt and tragic end. Convicted of a serious criminal offence which had nothing whatever to do with his work for the Federation, Morry Davis was sentenced to a term of imprisonment. His presidency of the Federation was of course terminated. On 2 January 1945 the General Council, over which the Vice-President (M. A. Glassman) presided, rescinded the resolutions of November and December 1940 and ordered fresh elections, which took place on 28 February. Although Davis subsequently attempted to regain office in the Federation, this breathtaking ambition was doomed to failure. He became a recluse and died in 1985, at the age of 89. In a carefully-worded obituary in the *Jewish Chronicle* (12 April 1985) Michael Goldman (Jung's successor as Federation Secretary) had this to say of him:

Although he played no part in the Federation's administration after 1945, I consulted him occasionally on communal matters and was impressed by his still acute grasp of Anglo-Jewry's problems.

[His] latter years were sadly marred by illness and loneliness — he was a bachelor without close relatives — and tribute is due to a few members of the

Stamford Hill Beth Hamedrash where he regularly davened, who befriended and cared for him.

How are we to summarise and evaluate the legacy of the Davis presidency? The man himself was a paradox: a socialist who brushed aside democratic principles; an Orthodox Jew who paid no attention to a Beth Din; a communal leader who applied the resources of the Federation to many worthy and altruistic purposes, but who at the same time seemed to have little regard for the Federation's public image, less still for its internal sensitivities. Did these paradoxes perhaps betray a tormented soul, and can we, in tracing the final extraordinary years of his rule, detect signs of the mental instability that afflicted him in later life?

In some important respects Davis left the Federation in a much stronger position than that which it had enjoyed in 1928. The charge later made against him - that he neglected to promote the interests of the Federation in the then outlying suburbs of London, to which Jews were relocating in ever larger numbers in the inter-war period – lacks substance. It must be remembered that at this time the Federation, unlike the United Synagogue, had no synagogues of its own: it was an organisation composed exclusively of legally independent congregations. It could of course offer financial help to embryo communities, but only if they wished to come within its ambit. As outlined in the previous chapter, a number did so. Some of the new suburban communities were at this time not particularly Orthodox. The Hendon congregation is a case in point here. At the same time – as the history of the Hendon community shows – the Federation did suffer from a bad image, but on account of the resignation of Louis Montagu rather than through the reputation of Morry Davis: in 1932 Hendon rejected the attractive terms offered by the Federation (which would have included almost complete autonomy) and joined the United Synagogue.

We must also bear in mind that Davis worked selflessly to preserve the Federation and to protect its interests during the Second World War, and that it was the war itself which posed the greatest threat to the Federation's well-being. It has been estimated that about 60,000 Jewish men and women were conscripted into the United Kingdom's armed forces. Many of these came from the East End, where the running of synagogues had to be left, perforce, to older generations. More serious still was the very necessary evacuation of children from the nation's capital. Under Davis the Federation responded warmly to appeals from Chief Rabbi Hertz and Dayan Abramsky for financial assistance in providing kosher food for evacuees. However, as Davis warned in November 1939, "the problem of *kashrut* cannot be separated, as some authorities are trying to do, from Jewish education. The problems must be faced as a whole and not piecemeal. Education without *kasher* food, however good the Hebrew instruction, would be a tragic farce, as the children are now living with non-Jews eating treifah food". As for those children remaining in London, Davis signalled his immediate intention to make special grants to enable Talmud Torahs to be reopened. At the same time, he announced that Federation members in the armed forces would continue to remain in benefit "without continuing their subscriptions". Secretary Jung represented the Federation on the Central Jewish Committee for Problems of Evacuation, to which the Federation contributed £450 to enable canteens to be opened where children could have all their meals during Passover. In addition, the Federation made the British government an interest-free loan of £5,000.

But the major blow suffered by the Federation as a result of the war was undoubtedly the large-scale destruction not merely of East London synagogues but of the communities that supported and used them. In November 1940, the General Council was informed that the Stepney Orthodox and Wellington Road synagogues had been totally destroyed by enemy action, that the Limehouse and Fieldgate Street synagogues had been "blasted", and that extensive damage had been caused to the Grove Street synagogue, Philpot Street Great, Nelson Street Sphardish and Congregation of Jacob (Commercial Road). Other Federation synagogues destroyed by the Nazis included Bethnal Green Great, Lambeth, and the Spital Square Synagogue in which the foundation meeting of the Federation had taken place. Both cemeteries – but particularly that at Edmonton – suffered bomb damage. The Federation maintained its headquarters in Leman Street but moved all its books and files not regularly required in London to an emergency office in Chesham, Buckinghamshire. Federation members who were evacuated were able to pay their subscriptions centrally.

Nonetheless, in spite of the superlative efforts undertaken by its staff and honorary officers to preserve the Federation of old, the permanent exodus of Jews from the East End was irreversible. Stepney's Jewish population declined from about 60,000 in 1940 to not more than 30,000 by 1945. At the end of the war the Federation comprised, on paper, some 70 congregations serving the needs of about 150,000 families. What proportion of these still lived in

Bomb Damage on Commercial Road c1942-c1943

the East End is uncertain; but it is evident that the proportion decreased as war-damaged and slum properties were cleared for redevelopment in the immediate post-war period. If the Federation was to survive at all after 1945, it could only do so in a radically altered form.

The problems resulting from the war and the changing demography of London Jewry were to form the central preoccupations of the Federation in the late 1940s and throughout the 1950s. But they were overshadowed, in 1945, by two even more urgent considerations: the lay and spiritual leaderships of the organisation.

The first engaged the attention also of Chief Rabbi Hertz, but for reasons which are still unclear. The elections which the General Council ordered at the beginning of 1945 resulted in the elevation to the presidency of Aaron Wright, a distinguished barrister then aged 40. Wright was one of the leading British Zionists of his generation; he held the chairmanships of the United Palestine Appeal and was President of the Jewish National Fund. He had been active in United Synagogue circles, and in March 1941 had incurred the displeasure of its leadership by editing a newsletter (only one issue of which ever appeared) to give expression to what Philip Goldberg, the United Synagogue's Secretary, termed his "extreme Nationalist views". Wright's Zionist activities had undoubtedly given him a high profile among Federation members, and were certain to make him popular with them. But he had never evinced any inclination to hold Federation office. His own version of the events by which he came to offer himself to the Federation as its President was published in 1970:

> The presidency of the Federation became vacant in 1944, for the first time since 1928. The Chief Rabbi, the late Dr. J. H. Hertz, requested me to see him and in his usual direct fashion told me it was my duty to become President of the Federation. I was both astonished and dismayed. I pointed out that I had taken no part in the Federation's activities, and I was already

carrying heavy communal responsibilities in the Jewish National Fund and the Joint Israel Appeal, in addition to an onerous wartime post in Government service. Dr. Hertz was not a man to take "No" for an answer and he pressed the matter. I think his motives were two-fold. He wished to strengthen the Federation as a bastion of Orthodox Judaism and mobilise its support for the Chief Rabbinate, and he was anxious to ensure that its leadership was in safe Zionist hands.

[C. Domb (Ed), Memories of Kopul Rosen (London, 1970), p.73]

This statement, so far as it bears upon Hertz's motives, needs to be critically examined. The Federation's commitment to Zionism was beyond question; in the post-Holocaust atmosphere of 1945 there was no possibility whatever of a non- or even lukewarm Zionist being elevated to its presidency. The supposition that Dr Hertz wished to "mobilise" the support of the Federation for the Chief Rabbinate is, however, likely to have been true, but in a very specific sense to which Aaron Wright did not allude. The presidency of the Federation was not offered to him. He had to contest it, and his opponent in this contest was Dr Bernard Homa, his "good friend", from whom he was divided "neither on public nor on personal issues".

Before the war Homa had crossed swords with Hertz over the latter's determination to certify the Liberal Jewish Synagogue (1935) as "a body of persons professing the Jewish religion". They had previously (1933) been in conflict over Hertz's unsuccessful attempt to have the licensing of shochetim centralised within the Chief Rabbinate. Homa had led the opposition to the autocracy of Morry Davis, and was himself an elected Labour member of the London County Council. His elevation to the presidency of the Federation was a prospect which Chief Rabbi Hertz did not welcome, and it seems likely that Hertz's central motive in approaching Aaron Wright was to secure at the head of the Federation a man whom he regarded as less formidable and certainly less likely to publicly challenge his authority. In the event, Wright defeated Homa but recognised the latter's great wisdom and the important Orthodox interests that he represented: on Wright's initiative (April 1946) the post of "Chairman" of the Federation was created for Homa to fill. "In the troubled times that lay ahead [Wright acknowledged in 1970] he was my chief ally".

Hertz may also have nurtured the hope that, under Aaron Wright, the Federation would acknowledge – at least *de facto* – the authority and paramountcy of his ecclesiastical office. But this was not to be. It is true that during the war, and because of the gravest of situations that faced world Jewry, the Federation had co-operated fully with and under Dr Hertz in coping with the many national and international emergencies that arose. But by the time of Hertz's death (14 January 1946) the Federation had already appointed its own religious head, and when Sir Robert Waley-Cohen, the President of the United Synagogue, requested the Federation "to give a lead to the country by agreeing to repose in Dayan [H. M.] Lazarus [the Acting Chief Rabbi] the same authority and regard him as the Spiritual Chief", the Executive of the Federation transmitted to the Jewish press a curt negative response.

Subsequent discussions between the Federation and the United Synagogue concerning the appointment of Hertz's successor took a predictable turn. Before agreeing to participate in the Electoral College that was to appoint a new Chief Rabbi, the Federation raised (as in 1912) the question of the basis of representation on the electing body. On 23 October 1947 the Executive of the Federation agreed to accept an offer from the United Synagogue that it be given ten representatives at a preliminary conference, to decide procedure. But on 4 November the Executive instructed those representatives "to demand proportional representation on the Electoral College ... and in the event of this demand not being acceded to they should withdraw from the Conference". The demand was of course rejected.

But, as it turned out, the actual grounds upon which the Federation did indeed withdraw were very different. Federation representatives raised with the United Synagogue the delicate question of the relationship between the Chief Rabbi and the Beth Din, maintaining (as before) that it was contrary to Orthodoxy for a Chief Rabbi to be able to over-rule the Dayanim, as was provided for in the United Synagogue's constitution. The Federation insisted that "a properly constituted and representative Beth Din shall be established"; that "consultation between the Chief Rabbi and this fully representative Beth Din shall take place on all matters of Jewish law and religious principles"; and that "any pronouncement on such matters shall be issued by the Chief Rabbi in accordance with the majority ruling of such a Beth Din". The United Synagogue would not agree to these conditions. Mr Abba Bornstein, of the *Machzike Hadass*, put the Federation's point of view very succinctly when he told its General Council (1 March 1948) that "A Rav in his own town might decide on halachic matters, but where there was a Beth Din the Rav was obliged to consult them. Jewish life knows of no papal infallibility".

So it was that the Federation played no part in the election of Israel Brodie as Chief Rabbi and paid nothing towards the upkeep of his office other than through the marriage authorisation fees. Significantly, in November 1947 the Federation had already discussed the possibility of establishing its own machinery for the certification of marriages, and had discussed the possibility of establishing its own Beth Din. It had, moreover, already made an appointment to the newly-created office of Principal Rabbi.

This had come about as the culmination of a debate within the General Council and the Executive in the summer of 1945. The Federation had been without a religious head since the death of Rabbi Jung in 1921. "In numbers [Aaron Wright later recorded] the Federation was still impressive ... But a number of its synagogues in the East End of London, formerly centres of great learning and fiery religious zeal, had become almost empty shells ... The need for inspiring leadership was pressing." Ideally, the Federation would have liked to appoint an outstanding Talmudic authority, steeped in the ways of the now-destroyed yeshivot of eastern Europe but able also (in Wright's phrase) "to make an impact on the present generation, to help in stimulating our Synagogues and the formation of new congregations and to deal with the problem of returning soldiers, youth problems and the many educational tasks now facing us". A search committee was charged with the task of finding such a person consulted Chief Rabbi Hertz, Dayan Abramsky, and the Rabbis Council of the Federation as well as Dr Isaac Herzog, the Ashkenazi Chief Rabbi of Mandate Palestine, and the renowned scholar Rabbi Meyer Berlin of Jerusalem. The committee reported (July 1945) that it seemed there was only one man who could combine all the necessary qualities, Rabbi Dr J. B. Soloveitchik of Boston, USA. But he was unwilling to accept the post.

It was therefore decided to make two appointments: a Talmudic authority "who would deal with problems of Din, Kashrus, Mikvah, higher Jewish education, and if it were possible to arrange, he would have a seat on the Beth Din"; and a Principal Rabbi, whose overall task it would be "to bring new vigour into the work of the Federation to enable the Federation to play a full and worthy part in the life of the Community". The first appointment was never made – though a number of strong candidates were considered. For the second, and on the recommendation of Dr Hertz, the Federation secured the services of the then Communal Rabbi of Glasgow, Dr Yaacov Kopul Rosen.

Kopul ("Cyril") Rosen (1913-62) was then just 31 years of age. A Londoner by birth, he had attended the Etz Chaim Yeshivah and from 1934 to 1938 had studied at the Mir Yeshivah, Poland, at which he gained *semicha*. In February 1939, he had become the first Rabbi of the Higher Crumpsall Hebrew Congregation, Manchester, and it was from the University of Manchester (1944) that he had received the degree of Master of Arts for a dissertation on "Rabbi Salanter and the Musar Movement". (Much later – 1959 - he was to receive a PhD from the University of London for a thesis on "The Concept of the Mitzvah"). It was also in 1944 that he had been appointed to the Glasgow post, which he retained for only 18 months before accepting appointment with the Federation of Synagogues. At that time he was already Vice-President of the British Mizrachi; he attained its Presidency in 1947.

Rosen's elevation as Principal Rabbi of the Federation was not achieved without opposition. He was not a great scholar and he was certainly not the saintly divine, of mature years, whom some felt would alone be fitted for such a position. There was a rather undignified opposition to him from the Federation's rabbinate, some members of which objected publicly to his title while others privately grumbled that so young a man should have been preferred over them. One rabbi lectured the General Council (22 October 1945) that "only a great Gaon should be chosen for such a distinguished post", but he was answered by the Treasurer (Jack Goldberg), who pointed out that "Immigration had ceased more or less completely, and it was therefore essential that the Federation should choose a man from their midst who would understand the psychology of the average English Jew". The appointment was unanimously approved.

Kopul Rosen's great talents lay in the fields of oratory, organisation and education. He was a man of action rather than a philosopher, though he had in fact thought and written a great deal about the problem that he regarded as central to the post-Holocaust survival of Anglo-Jewry, namely how to foster a love of (and therefore the practice of) Judaism in a community that was fast becoming secularised and alienated. The synagogue he viewed as a means to an end rather than an end in itself: for of what use were synagogues if there were no worshippers to fill them? In a pamphlet that was – and was doubtless meant to be – controversial, published by the Federation in August 1946, and entitled *The Future of the Federation of Synagogues*, Rosen sketched both the problem and his solution to it.

He began by making a severely practical but at the same time utterly realistic statement, that "we [the Federation] have not the machinery, neither the personnel, nor the resources to tackle all the problems which face London Jewry today". If the Federation was to be nothing more than "another synagogal body", merely duplicating functions performed elsewhere, its continued existence could not be justified. But if it conducted itself as "a Jewish kehilla dealing with Jewish life in all its aspects", then it might have "a great future". Rosen referred in this connection to the memorandum (of which he was in fact the author) that the Federation had recently presented to the Anglo-American Commission of Enquiry on Palestine: "The Federation thus demonstrated its interest and association not only with Anglo-Jewry but with Judaism and Jewry in the widest sense."

The pamphlet then proceeded to identify "two major tasks which confront our community as a whole ... The first task is to reclaim the large masses of Jews who have drifted away from Judaism and who remain attached to the community by the slenderest threads of sentiment and emotion ... They are the rootless Jews of our community. There is another section, perhaps smaller in number, which represent a somewhat different problem ... There are thousands of young men and women ... who were reared in the atmosphere of Jewish learning and strict observance ... I am convinced that the future of Anglo-Jewish life will be moulded by them ... their problem is how to retain the indispensable core given to them by their parents, in the modern environment in which they find themselves".

Rosen insisted that because the Federation did not have to hand the resources to tackle both problems, it must concentrate on one only. He therefore urged that "we must endeavour to cater for those Jews whose parents established the Federation, and who themselves feel an attachment to all that is covered by that very wide term 'Yiddishkeit'". "Let us [he continued] do a limited task well, rather than a colossal task badly."

The Future of the Federation of Synagogues was much more than a prospectus for the Federation itself. In a few pages, Rosen identified the major problems faced by Anglo-Jewry in the aftermath of the Holocaust. Synagogues, he argued, would only be filled once people were motivated to fill them. The *Beth Hamedrash* [House of Learning] was a much more useful communal institution. "It is my fervent desire that wherever the Federation acquires a building, it will be opened as a Beth Hamedrash." Rosen also called for an enhanced status for the Federation rabbinate, whose members had not in the past "been given the opportunity ... to exert that influence upon the community which they can, and desire to, exert". He also drew an important distinction between rabbis and ministers of religion who were not rabbinically qualified. The Federation certainly possessed rabbinic scholars, but they were "almost exclusively confined to the East End of London". As East End synagogues merged, these men (he argued) should be relocated into the suburban communities. In most of the Jewish youth clubs and movements then to be found in the metropolis Rosen doubted that such scholars could have any influence, because these centres flourished without any "religious environment". But he seemed to favour the reconstitution of the old Sinai League, to encourage the study of Torah, and he expressed the hope that the Federation might encourage the establishment of adult study circles throughout London. Finally, and in order to facilitate the programme he had put forward, Rosen called for an elevation of the status of the Federation at the expense of the "local patriotism and parochial interests" of individual affiliated congregations.

Kopul Rosen's pamphlet at once became a subject of intense controversy. Taken as a whole, the ideas it encompassed envisaged a role for the Federation which – so it was said – catered for a religiously-inclined elite at the expense of the mass membership. The Federation would move gradually from the East End to the suburbs where, as a unitary rather than a federal body, it would devote its resources to the spiritual needs of the few. Of course, Rosen stressed time and again that this would merely be a means to an end. The few, in turn, would influence the many: the Federation would become the power-house, fuelling a religious revival.

These ideas (which were later to find a very different expression – though with the same general end in view – in Rosen's foundation of Carmel College) had the support of Aaron Wright and other Honorary Officers, but they met with strong opposition elsewhere in the Federation hierarchy. Requests from the Principal Rabbi for additional funding for the Federation rabbinate were not enthusiastically received. Rosen, Wright and Bernard Homa strongly supported the establishment late in 1945 of the London Board for Jewish Religious Education (LBJRE), which it was hoped would be able to provide a cadre of qualified teachers both for religion classes attached to synagogues and for 'withdrawal' classes in state schools. The LBJRE was to be financed communally, through taxation imposed by the parent bodies, of which the Federation (at the instigation of Dayan Abramsky) was one. In this way, Talmud Torahs would no longer lead a hand-to-mouth existence, dependent upon the charity of the synagogues to which they were attached; and teachers of a higher calibre would be attracted by better and more reliable scales of remuneration.

The United Synagogue agreed to impose upon its members an education tax equivalent to one-third of membership contributions. The Federation could do no less and, indeed, the Joint Finance Committee of the Federation and its Burial Society agreed in April 1946 to make immediate grants of £5,000 (£2,000 of which was an outright gift) to the new body, in advance of the tax being levied. But the tax was not well received by the wider Federation membership that was being asked to pay it. Moreover, since the Federation synagogues were autonomous, the tax could not be imposed upon them, other than through an increase in burial fees; in the immediate post-war period it was felt that to take such a step might lead to mass resignations, since an increasing number of Federation members who lived in the suburbs retained their membership of East End synagogues only because of relatively low membership rates.

This fear was probably unfounded, and certainly did not materialise in August 1950 when, on the initiative of one of the Treasurers of the Burial Society – Morris Lederman – the General Council doubled the contribution rate to the Society in order to raise more money for the LBJRE. But in 1946 some opposition to the tax, and to other reforms then being carried through, appears to have prompted the then Treasurer, M. J. Turner, into an act of open defiance of Aaron Wright's leadership, for he refused to sign certain documents and cheques in connection with the transfer of moneys from the Burial Society into the main Federation accounts. This crisis, which Wright resolved by using the authority of his office to overrule the Treasurer, had less to do with the education tax, however, than with more fundamental – and more painful – decisions which the Federation was being asked to take at that time.

Kopul Rosen's suggestion, that the Federation should undergo a constitutional transformation, had echoed the views of Aaron Wright and Bernard Homa, that the days of the Federation as a loose-knit patchwork of small but legally independent bodies were numbered. The many problems inherent in coping with post-war reconstruction were clearly too great to be undertaken by a large number of separate synagogues, most of them clustered in that part of London that had suffered most heavily from the ravages of war. In any case, the war itself had accelerated the movement of Jews from the East End. An increasing number of Federation synagogues in east London had memberships that were actually located for the most part in the north-west and north-east suburbs: in Ilford, Hendon and Edgware and – though to a much lesser extent – in localities south of the River Thames. In the absence of some wealthy benefactor – a latter day Samuel Montagu perhaps – the resources necessary to build synagogues in these areas could only be found by contracting the scale of Federation activities in Whitechapel and Bethnal Green.

But as long as Jews continued to live in significant numbers in the East End, such a transfer of resources was bound to be resisted, partly on grounds of self-interest, partly on grounds of pure sentiment, sometimes (it must be said) on grounds of simple prejudice, itself religious or socio-economic in origin. Those Jews of modest means still living in the East End were not prepared to stand idly by and watch the funds of the Federation – funds which they and their parents had built up – used for the construction of comparatively luxurious houses of worship in comparatively affluent areas. At the same time many Federation members who had moved and were to move to these areas maintained their membership of East End synagogues either through a sense of spiritual loyalty or because it was financially advantageous to do so: membership rates were invariably lower in small East End synagogues free of the burden of heavy debt repayments. Moreover, because they were legally independent, and because of the then constitutional structure of the Federation, these East End synagogues were able to virtually dictate Federation policy: if funds were to be made available for the growing suburban communities, this had to be on terms acceptable to the East End, and these terms invariably included the continued support of many more separate East End congregations than were really necessary for the depleted Jewish communities still resident there.

With the advantage of hindsight, it is easy to say that in the immediate post-war years there ought to have been a drastic contraction of Federation activity in the East End. Given the legal structure of the Federation in 1945, this was just not practicable. Aaron Wright did however address himself to the problem of Federation control over individual congregations, and in so doing began a process of fundamental constitutional change. Kopul Rosen's appointment as Principal Rabbi provided the opportunity and the excuse. Rosen did not wish to live in the East End. Wright therefore proposed that the Federation purchase, as a synagogue for him, the premises of the West Hampstead Congregational Church, Finchley Road. The site was not ideal, placed as it was near the junction of Finchley Road and Platts Lane, practically at the border of West Hampstead and Cricklewood and over a mile from the centre of Golders Green, where the United Synagogue had been established as long ago as 1922 and into which there had been a large migration not only of Jews from inner London but also of Jewish refugees from central Europe. Nonetheless, at a purchase price of £12,500 the building (which included a communal hall) was a bargain, and it gave the Federation a foothold in one of the principal new areas of Jewish settlement in the metropolitan suburbs.

A nucleus of Federation members existed in the neighbourhood of the West Hampstead synagogue, of which Julius Jung acted as temporary secretary. But the purchase moneys had of necessity to be provided out of the Federation's own funds. In order to underpin this financial interest, and to exercise a much tighter control over the synagogue's finances, the constitutional relationship between the synagogue and the Federation differed fundamentally from that of all the then-existing affiliated congregations. The synagogue of course elected a full complement of honorary officers and a committee to oversee its religious, educational and social activities. But all moneys contributed by its members were to be paid centrally into the Federation, and the Federation was responsible for sanctioning all outgoings. The West Hampstead congregation was not, therefore, independent; whilst day-to-day activities remained under local supervision, ultimate managerial authority rested with the Federation, through its General Council and the Joint Finance Committee of the Federation and its Burial Society.

The West Hampstead Synagogue thus became the first "Constituent" synagogue of the Federation. In accordance with a policy approved by the General Council in October 1946, all constituent synagogues were to be given Hebrew names. That at West Hampstead became the *Shomrei Hadath*; during the High Holydays that year it attracted 250 worshippers. In addition to Rabbi Rosen the synagogue acquired the services of the Reverence F. Rosenberg as Reader and of Rabbi J. H. Gordon as Second Reader and Teacher. The establishment of other constituent communities quickly followed. A building was acquired in Chamberlayne Road, Willesden; as the *Ohel Shem* it was consecrated on 24 November 1946, and the Reverend J. J. Kacenelenbogen was appointed its Reader. Meanwhile a group of Federation members living in Edgware, under the leadership of Abraham Olivestone, had begun to hold services in a church hall, where a weekly *shiur* was conducted by Rabbi Rappaport. A site at Stonegrove was purchased for £6,250, but the construction of a purpose-built synagogue there had to await government permission under post-war building controls. Consequently, although as the Edgware Beth Hamedrash it was admitted into the Federation as a constituent in September 1946, the *Yeshurun* synagogue built at Stonegrove was not opened unto some four years later.

The *Shomrei Hadath*, *Ohel Shem* and *Yeshurun* congregations, plus the Maida Vale Beth Hamedrash (a house in Elgin Avenue the lease of which was bought by the Federation for £4,800, and which was named the *Emet v'Shalom* Synagogue in June 1948) comprised the founding group of constituent synagogues of the Federation. Their establishment necessitated a major revision of the Federation's constitution, ratified at a special meeting of the General Council on 1 June 1947. The new constitution embodied a series of bye-laws setting out the mode of government of constituent synagogues and their financial subordination to the Federation; the General Council itself was suitably enlarged to include the president and the financial representative of each constituent (with provision for more representation if membership exceeded one hundred male members); the president of each constituent synagogue was to sit as of right on the Federation's Executive, and the financial representative also became an Executive member if this membership figure was exceeded. The prices at which seats in constituent synagogues were rented were to be fixed by local boards of management, subject to Federation approval. Supplementary laws adopted by the General Council on 24 May 1948 provided for each constituent congregation to submit to head office an annual budget of projected income and expenditure, for General Council approval. These supplementary laws also made it clear that the power to appoint all officials of constituent synagogues lay with the Federation, though subject naturally to close consultation with individual congregations.

The adoption of the 1947 constitution marked a watershed in the history of the Federation, and not just on account of the provisions it contained for constituent synagogues – with all that these provisions implied for the future relationship between the central decision-making bodies of the Federation and the local communities that were part of it. As the many small affiliated congregations became defunct, or amalgamated, and as the number of constituent synagogues grew, the balance of power within the federal body was bound to change, and in a way that would provide for much less local autonomy and much more central control. Put another way, the Federation of Synagogues would become what the United Synagogue was, at least in organisational sense. This scenario bore the strong imprint of Aaron Wright, who freely and publicly acknowledged (at the General Council, 1 June 1947), "with gratitude the considerable assistance received from the United Synagogue in the drafting of the [new] Constitution".

Within a few weeks, however, Wright was no longer the Federation's President – even though he had been voted back into that office at the elections held immediately the new constitution had come into force. In *Memories of Kopul Rosen* Wright explained that at the July 1947 election of Honorary Officers and Executive, he and Bernard Homa "felt strongly that it was essential to elect people who could work reasonably together ... Homa and I agree to stand for re-election and recommended a list for the various offices to be filled ... The General Council proceeded to re-elect Homa and myself and with conspicuous lack of realism rejected with equal enthusiasm almost all those we had nominated ... Homa and I considered that we had no alternative but to resign". This they did. Subsequently, early in 1948, Jack Goldberg was elected as the Federation's fifth President, together with Jack Slutsky as a Vice-President in place of Homa. Later that year (one of the most eventful in post-1945 Anglo-Jewish history, for it witnessed the Declaration of the State of Israel and the election of Israel Brodie as Chief Rabbi), Carmel College – the UK's first and only Jewish boarding school – was opened. Kopul Rosen had been devoting an increasing amount of time to this venture, and to work for Israel. On 8 February 1949 he, too, resigned from the Federation, irritated by what he regarded as its introspection and disenchanted that it had not demonstrated more enthusiasm for travelling down the highways he had designated for it.

Aaron Wright's account of the circumstances leading to his own resignation was true. But it was not the whole truth. On 17 June 1947 the Executive had agreed, by 12 votes to 2, to endorse his proposal that the General Council be asked to elect him as President, Dr Homa and Mr A. Mann as Vice-Presidents (the office of Chairman having been abolished), Messrs A. Glassman and L. Grahame as Treasurers of the Burial Society and Messrs A. Bornstein and A. B. Olivestone as Federation Treasurers. Wright was adamant in his refusal to countenance the election as Honorary Officers of Mr Turner and of David Galinski. Turner had (it will be recalled) declined to sign certain documents and cheques in connection with the transfer of funds from the Burial Society to the Federation; but he had done so on the solid grounds that the prior consent of the respective Finance Committees had not been obtained. He and Galinski (also a Federation Treasurer and the much-respected Vice-President of the Stamford Hill Beth Hamedrash and Acting President of the *Etz Chaim* Yeshivah) were fearful of Aaron Wright's mode of governance and objected to it; in September 1946, for example, Wright had appointed an Accountant, at a salary of £500 per annum, without asking for prior approval from the Executive. The views of Turner and Galinski evidently commanded support, for it was Turner who was elected a Vice-President in 1947 (and not Mann), and it was Galinski (and not Grahame) who was elected to a Treasurership.

Wright's virtual demand, that the General Council elect his nominees, had certainly backfired and was itself evidence of – at the very least – a serious insensitivity to its wishes. But we may detect, in the rejection of his demand, an undercurrent of anxiety arising partly out of the direction in which he was leading the Federation but more deeply out of the pace at which this change of direction was being undertaken, and the burdens which it was placing upon Federation finances. Reference has already been made to opposition to the education levy. The parlous financial state of the LBJRE necessitated further injections of cash from its parent bodies. In October 1946 Wright was able to persuade the General Council to agree that repayment of the £3,000 advance made to the LBJRE be postponed and that, from April 1947, any surpluses received from the London Board of Shechita be made over to it. The Executive also wished the LBJRE to receive the proceeds of the Tombstone Tax imposed by the Federation Burial Society, but apparently this proposal, though implemented, was never put to the General Council.

The foundation and running of constituent synagogues inevitably placed further burdens upon headquarters staff, who were having to cope with the many problems arising from the need to reorganise and rationalise the structure of Federation communities in the East End. Nor should it be thought that the growth and funding of constituent congregations precluded either the establishment of new or the refurbishment of existing affiliated synagogues. In December 1945 it was agreed to advance £1,500 to the members of the Bethnal Green Great Synagogue to enable them to buy the building they were using as a place of worship in Chance Street. In 1948 the Federation gave an interest-free loan of £1,000 to the North-West London (now the *Sinai*) Synagogue, Golders Green, to enable it to buy the site it had rented hitherto. Premises in Shacklewell Lane were purchased for the use of members of the bombed Wellington Road synagogue. A group of Federation members who had moved out of the East End to Croydon successfully applied for an interest-free loan of £3,000 to buy a property in Addiscombe suitable for use as a place of worship. The Letchworth Hebrew Congregation was admitted to affiliate status (1946), as was the Highbury Synagogue (1947), and the Oxford Jewish community entered into an agreement with the Federation (also 1947) for burial purposes.

Throughout the late 1940s the Federation continued to make a wide variety of charitable donations, especially to refugee and Zionist causes; in May 1948 the sum of £2,000 was given to the State of Israel. In June 1946 the General Council agreed to make the sum of £1,500 available from the Burial

Society to finance the work of the *Va'ad HaRabbonim*. At the same meeting the sum of £2,000 was contributed to the London Board of Mikvaot. At the end of the war the provision of Mikvaot in London, for the observance of the laws relating to Family Purity, was very inadequate. There was one private mikvah in the East End, only two in north London (one private, the other attached to the Stamford Hill Beth Hamedrash, a Federation affiliate), and a private mikvah in Cricklewood. On Kopul Rosen's initiative the London Board of Mikvaot was established, with Dr Jacob Braude (of the Union of Orthodox Hebrew Congregations) as its honorary secretary. Braude was the prime mover in the building of the North-West London Communal Mikvah, constructed in Hendon in 1946. Three years later the Federation donated another £1,500 to the Mikvaot Board, and additionally agreed to make the sum of £1,500 available towards the construction of a communal mikvah in the East End; this building, in Dunk Street, was consecrated by Chief Rabbi Brodie in June that year.

To cope with all this extra activity and to service a plethora of sub-committees (Constitution, Membership, Cemeteries, Property, Education) the Federation's staff was expanded. At the end of the war this staff, working in the increasingly cramped offices at 64 Leman Street, consisted of the Secretary (Julius Jung), a book-keeper, three clerks, one telephonist and one shorthand-typist. The appointment of an Accountant has already been noted. In May 1946 the headmaster of the Jewish Day School in Willesden, H. Lewis, began an 18-month appointment as Joint Secretary to relieve Jung of some of the burdens of his office. At the same time the Principal Rabbi was provided with an office of his own, and a secretary, at 19 Leman Street. Kopul Rosen also had a car put at his disposal.

As a result of the many new tasks undertaken by the Federation at this time, its expenditure increased substantially. In 1946 this expenditure totalled some £9,000. The grant of 25 per cent of Burial Society contributions agreed upon in 1921, and which had made the Federation self-supporting, now brought in only £2,500 per annum. On 6 February 1947 the Executive agreed that the resultant deficit of £6,500 would be made good by the Burial Society henceforth paying over to the Federation the sum of £500 each month. Once again, therefore, the funds of the Burial Society had been 'raided' to service other activities. The use of burial contributions was a time-honoured method of raising money for communal purposes: like shechita fees, subscriptions to burial societies have long been a form of communal taxation. What seems to have caused dissension within the Federation in the late 1940s was not so much, therefore, the device itself as the fact that it was being deployed to facilitate controversial initiatives. For while the uses to which Federation money was being put – such as the establishment and maintenance of synagogues in the suburbs - were in themselves entirely laudable, the claims of the East End seemed to be being undervalued in the process.

We cannot be certain what proportion of Federation members still lived in the East End at this time. A calculation based upon the figures given in the preceding paragraph would seem to indicate that in 1947 membership of the Burial Society stood at approximately 11,500. This figure naturally excludes those members of Federation synagogues who for one reason or another chose not to belong to its Burial Society – perhaps because they paid burial fees to a Jewish friendly society. In April 1947, in connection with the abortive negotiations with the United Synagogue concerning Federation participation in the election of a Chief Rabbi, Aaron Wright declared the total membership of all Federation synagogues to be about 15,000. This figure represented an increase of some 2,000 upon that given by Cecil Roth in his 1937 history of the Federation but – as Wright was candid enough to admit – it was still now less than the United Synagogue's 20,000 male seat-holders. At the 15 April 1947 General Council meeting Morris Lederman alleged that "25% of the Federation members had joined the United Synagogue against their will because at that time they had no Federation Synagogue in their districts". By 1950 male membership of the United Synagogue exceeded 25,000. It seems reasonable to infer that much of this increase, which was derived from the suburban communities, was made up of defecting members of the Federation, some of whom, however, continued their membership of the Federation's Burial Society.

It also seems reasonable to delineate the following groupings within the Federation in the late 1940s: a group that had moved (in the main) into the northern, north-western and north-eastern suburbs of London, but who were anxious to retain their Federation connections because of lower membership rates attaching to East End synagogues; another group, living in the same areas, whose members preferred to see the establishment of Federation synagogues in these localities and who lobbied for a transfer of resources for this purpose; and a group of diminishing size (but still amounting to perhaps over half the Federation's total membership in 1945) who, so long as they remained resident in the East End, wished to see a strong Federation presence maintained there, not least because it seemed to them highly unlikely that Jews would not for the foreseeable future continue to live in the East End in large numbers. The first group had a diminishing interest in the Federation, but the second and third groups fought with each other for the better part of a decade until, by natural demographic processes, the former triumphed over the latter.

Amalgamations of East End synagogues were taking place well before 1939 (as we noted in the previous chapter), but at a relatively leisurely pace. During the 1930s no less than three congregations in Christian Street amalgamated with nearby communities - but not, it is worth stressing, with each other, a sign perhaps of the intense parochial rivalry that was so marked a feature of East End Federation entities. The Little Alie Street and Jubilee Street synagogues merged, as did those at Whitechapel Road and Vine Court, Fieldgate Street Sphardish and Settles Street, the Glory of Jacob and Mile End New Town, the Plotzker and Great Alie Street, and the Voice of Jacob and King Edward Street. However, the 1939-45 war made further, large-scale amalgamations an overriding necessity.

Although it was natural that the many small, close-knit synagogues of the East End should regret the inevitability of their own closure, the demographic reality was so stark, even in 1945, that it could not be avoided. Where Federation members had moved out of the East End but into areas where there were other Federation congregations (for example Stoke Newington, Hackney, Walthamstow, Neasden), the Laws of the Burial Society permitted transfer without hindrance or penalty. Some East End synagogues attempted to confront this situation by refusing transfer facilities. One speaker told a meeting of the Finance Committee on 12 April 1945 that "the Great Garden Street Synagogue had received applications for hundreds of transfers but had refused them all. It would ruin the East End Synagogues were such transfers granted". But, as Aaron Wright pointed out, to refuse a transfer was unconstitutional. Besides (he pointed out), "Synagogues would not be kept together by such means. East End Jewry was dwindling in numbers rapidly and nothing would stop the eventual closing of many East End Synagogues. A much better scheme would be to arrange the amalgamation of a number of Synagogues giving the remaining Synagogues increased membership and financial strength and thus helping them to carry on".

The Federation was slow to take this advice. It was agreed, by 16 votes to 7, to grant any request for transfer, subject of course to any arrears of contributions being settled and to "an attempt being [made] to persuade the applicant for transfer to remain a member of the Synagogue". This deliberate fudging of the issue provided only a temporary respite. Meanwhile, the problem was being compounded by two other factors. First, the policy of establishing constituent synagogues in the suburbs ran counter to that of persuading members in these areas to retain their links with East End communities. Second, the priority placed by the post-war Labour government upon building houses and factories meant that synagogues which had been destroyed or badly damaged remained unrebuilt and unrepaired: the managements existed, but the physical structures did not. Lured by the prospect of substantial war-damage claims in respect of properties that were legally theirs (and not the

Federation's), the honorary officers and trustees of these synagogues were not inclined to amalgamate themselves out of existence; but they could not offer any facility to their congregants beyond that of Burial Society membership.

Discussions with presidents of East End synagogues did bear some fruit. An Amalgamation Committee was established, and through its good offices some mergers were effected: Greenfield Road with Vine Court; Artillery Lane with Ezras Chaim; the Roumanian Synagogue with Philpot Street Sphardish; the Lubiner & Lomzer with Fieldgate Street. In December 1947, the Executive approved a resolution to the effect that "all small Federation Synagogues who have no Rabbi or Chazan be barred from taking on any new members for the Federation Burial Society". But these steps did not address the nub of the problem – namely the gross over-provision of synagogues in the East End - to which in the late 1940s others were added: was the Federation to distribute resources evenly between the East End and the constituent synagogues in the

Great Garden Street Synagogue c1950–c1965

suburbs, or was it to engage in a deliberate policy of discrimination and – if so – in what direction and in what magnitude?

These major challenges formed the preoccupying themes of Jack Goldberg's presidency. He was unable to overcome them. A well-known communal worker and a valued member of the Defence and Finance committees of the Board of Deputies, he was accustomed to operate within a hierarchical command structure, whereas the office of President of the Federation of Synagogues, especially at this time, was more like that of a tightrope-walker. Moreover, though he had undoubted talents, their impact was blunted by his poor health and compromised by the circumstances of his election. Following Aaron Wright's resignation, three candidates had emerged for the presidency. The strongest was Dr Homa, but his policy of closer co-operation with the Union of Orthodox Hebrew Congregations – perhaps resulting in the establishment of a new Beth Din and Board of Shechita – had met with stiff resistance from the General Council. Morris Lederman, the third candidate, was popular but – having just turned 40 years of age – he did not possess Jack Goldberg's seniority. Goldberg won the three-cornered contest, but he seems in reality to have been everyone's second choice.

Within a short time of his becoming President of the Federation, Goldberg was also elected a Treasurer of the LBJRE. Due to the failure of the voluntary Education Tax the LBJRE was effectively bankrupt. Goldberg wished the Federation to play a more active part in its revival by trebling the weekly Burial contribution (from four pence to one shilling) and abolishing the tax as such: the Federation would thus finance the LBJRE through the Burial Society (to the extent of one-third of the weekly contribution) and at the same time raise extra revenue for its own use. By 12 votes to 4 the proposal was defeated (23 December 1948). Early the following year a less ambitious recommendation was put to the Executive: to permit the Education Tax to remain voluntary but nonetheless to double the Burial contribution, in order to make more money available for new congregations. This, too, received a hostile reception from some sections of the Executive, one member (M. Cooper) declaring that "The Executive had done nothing for the East End". Goldberg used his casting vote to ensure the motion's adoption – but it was never put to the General Council.

On the General Council the East End congregations had an overwhelming majority. What did Jack Goldberg and his supporters propose to do for them? Julius Jung had been asked to prepare a Memorandum on this subject, which was presented to and discussed by the General Council on 10 March 1949. Jung envisaged an expenditure of many thousands of pounds "with the object of revitalising East End Jewry". To further this end a Planning Committee was to be established to enquire "into all the causes of the present spiritual disintegration of our Synagogues in the East End of London". Negotiations were to be opened with the London County Council and Stepney Borough Council to find a site upon which a fairly large constituent synagogue could be built to replace the many small affiliated ones destroyed or damaged, or which would certainly be demolished as the East End was rebuilt. And steps were to be taken to restart the old Sinai Association and to establish Modern Hebrew classes.

How seriously was this Memorandum meant to be taken? We need to ask this question because the Memorandum's ambitious undertone was quite at variance with the harsh realities of East End Jewish life. Stepney Borough Council and the London County Council had by the end of 1949 told the Federation what its Honorary Officers must surely have already known: that no more than a dozen synagogues were sufficient for the whole of the East End. Contraction, not expansion, was what was needed. Such funds as were required to assist this process would come from the proceeds of synagogue disposals, war-damage claims, and compulsory-purchase compensation moneys. The only part of Jung's proposals that was ever substantially acted upon was the appointment of a young rabbi (J. Newman) to undertake youth work in the East End and to establish post-Barmitzvah classes. Newman initiated some useful work in contacting headteachers of local schools regarding children not attending Talmud Torah or religion classes. The Sinai Association was indeed reformed, using the premises of the Congregation of Jacob Synagogue, Commercial Road. But Newman's appointment terminated in the summer of 1950. He was not replaced.

Jack Goldberg was re-elected President in June 1949, but in the months that followed the suspicion grew stronger that he was less than totally committed to the East End. A section of the Executive, led by Mr Cooper, grew ever more vociferous in opposing what they regarded as a sell-out of the vital interests of East End Jewry, and whenever proposals were forthcoming to increase Federation income, this opposition demanded to know how much of it would be used for East End purposes. When, in October 1949, Jack Goldberg again asked the Executive to recommend a doubling of the Burial contribution (which had not been increased since 1921), and that the Education Tax be made compulsory, Cooper warned that "if the recommendations were approved there would be [a] tremendous outcry in East London".

Debate on the subject was adjourned, but resumed the following month on the basis of the earlier proposal to treble the contribution and apply one third of this sum (four pence per member) to the needs of Hebrew education, as determined by the General Council. The Executive Committee's debate on this proposition witnessed a hardening of attitudes on both sides. Cooper, again opposing the recommendation, warned that "Members of the East End would ... strongly oppose an increase in the contributions which might be used in part to help erecting Synagogues and pay high salaries for people in the North-West London area". Another speaker (M. Goldman) "felt very strongly that the Federation had no right to use the funds of the Burial Society for building Synagogues. If money is to be used for such purposes, it must be found by other means". But others spoke eloquently against this narrow view. Abraham Olivestone warned ominously that "were the Federation to discontinue with their present scheme of putting up Synagogues in outlying districts it would find within a number of years that it will have shrunk to a minor organisation".

By the narrowest of margins (9 votes to 7) the Executive approved the recommendation, and in January 1950 gave its blessing to a proposal to establish a Pension Fund for the Rabbonim and Chazanim of affiliated synagogues. The establishment of such a fund was, by common consent, long overdue; participation in it would entail the payment of a very modest membership fee (£5 per annum) by each affiliated congregation but, as Mr Slutsky pointed out, the very existence of the Fund would "introduce a contractual obligation for the first time between each [affiliated] Synagogue and Head Office". At the same time the Executive gave unanimous approval to a plan to amalgamate all Federation-affiliated East End places of worship into seventeen synagogues.

But those on the Executive who supposed that the opposition had melted away were deeply misled. When the plan was put to the General Council (9 March 1950), to treble Burial contributions, and to apply part of the proceeds to educational purposes and to the Pension Fund, there was uproar. The meeting was adjourned, and resumed on 18 April when a motion calling for Slutsky's resignation was carried by 67 votes to 46. Julius Jung's minute of this meeting records dramatically that "The President at this stage rose to say that he had come to the decision that his health was dearer to him than any organisation. In consequence of this, he wished the Council to accept his resignation".

Immediately thereafter, when tempers had had a chance to cool, there were calls on all sides for Jack Goldberg to reconsider his decision. But a motion expressing full confidence in him and his fellow honorary officers, though put to the General Council (25 April) with the full backing of the Executive, failed to pass (the voting was 42 in favour and 50 against). On 2 May 1950 Morris Lederman was voted into the chair of the Executive Committee, and it was he who presided over the Council meeting (28 August) at which a proposal to increase Burial contributions from four pence to eight pence per week – the increase to be used for educational purposes – was carried without a single vote being recorded against it.

Jack Goldberg died on 16 June 1951. He was just 57 years of age. That same month Morris Lederman was elected President of the Federation of Synagogues in his own right.

CHAPTER FIVE

A Kehilla – At Last

Morris Lederman (1908 – 2001) assumed the presidency of the Federation at a moment of great crisis – a much greater crisis, in truth, than that which had led to the resignation of Louis Montagu, or that which had accompanied the last years of the Davis regime. In 1950 the continued existence of the Federation was in doubt because of profound disagreements focussed on the very nature of the organisation. Did its future still lie primarily in the East End, serving the real needs of a dislocated and dwindling Jewish presence, and devoting its resources largely if not exclusively to these ends? Those who answered in the affirmative, and who expected the Jewish communities of the suburbs to establish their own places of worship, as the founding communities of the Federation had done, seem to have forgotten both the generosity of Samuel Montagu and the existence – now - of a United Synagogue whose ambience was much more attractive to the children and grandchildren of the immigrant generations.

But those who answered negatively often failed to recognise the extreme sensitivity of the East End, especially in the immediate post-Holocaust years, and in the wake of the re-establishment of the Jewish State. In the inter-war period East End Jewry had been a centre of Zionist activity and a repository of Torah-true Judaism. However, most Orthodox Jews who had fled from Nazism to England looked not to the Federation but to the Union of Orthodox Hebrew Congregations. The focus of Zionist activity was now no longer in London or even New York, but Jerusalem and Tel Aviv. Conscientious Jews who remained in the East End had therefore to come to terms with a much diminished status. This made them all the more determined to exercise whatever rights remained to them and to assert themselves to the fullest possible extent.

Morris Lederman succeeded in re-orientating the Federation without alienating the East End, or indeed any significant section of the collectivity of Federation communities. He was both an immigrant and an East Ender. Born in Mezeritz (some 60 miles south-east of Warsaw), he had come to London with his family when just twelve years old, as part of that often forgotten generation of Jewish emigrants who left an increasingly ultra-nationalist independent Poland in the aftermath of the Great War. The family eventually settled in Shore Road, between Bethnal Green and central Hackney, and worshipped at the North-East London Beth Hamedrash, Ainsworth Road. In this way Lederman had his first contact with the world of the Federation, and forged links that became stronger when he attended the Etz Chaim Yeshiva and trained as a shochet – a profession he followed for almost 28 years.

Lederman did not seek out high office in the Federation. He was, rather, sought out by others who saw in him a man with a great deal of common sense – a maker of peace rather than a deliverer of ultimatums, someone who listened a great deal and who could on occasion talk sharply to the rank-and-file, though never *at* them. Elected to the General Council in 1941, Lederman had risen quickly through its ranks. In 1946 he was elected one of the six

Federation representatives on Board of Deputies of British Jews, and two years later became one of the Treasurers of the Federation's Burial Society. Later that year, as Chairman of the Finance Sub-Committee, he supervised the planning of a superannuation scheme for senior head-office officials and rabbis and chazanim of constituent synagogues. In the aftermath of Aaron Wright's resignation he was elected to a Vice-Presidency of the Federation and practically assumed the role of acting president following Jack Goldberg's resignation in 1950. His formal election as President reflected the confidence shown in him by East Enders and 'suburbanites' alike. His very long tenure of this position would seem to indicate that this confidence was not misplaced. But – as we shall see – it permitted him to rule as an oligarch, with dire consequences that remained for too long hidden from public view.

The agreement of the General Council in August 1950 to raise Burial contributions in order to fund educational work was an early affirmation that the East End would accept from Lederman that which it had not been willing to countenance when proposed by others. There was another side to this agreement. Immediately upon assuming the chairmanship of the Executive Committee Lederman had had two meetings with the East End leadership. As a result, the old Amalgamation Committee (resented as an instrument of central direction) was absorbed within a new Planning Committee, chaired by one of the most articulate of East End spokesmen, Joseph Cymerman (of the Cannon Street Road synagogue); its terms of reference were "to tackle the urgent problem of bringing back to the London Jewish Community a full religious and cultural life, with particular and immediate attention to the East End, the cradle of the Federation".

The establishment of the Planning Committee, upon which all the larger East End affiliated congregations were represented, in effect placed the responsibility for the East End into its own hands. The committee managed to persuade some synagogues to withdraw applications for building and rebuilding licences and to agree, tentatively, to pool resources in order to construct one larger central place of worship. On 3 April 1951 Cymerman presented to the Executive a Memorandum, drafted by the Planning Committee, in which it was made clear that this large synagogue would have constituent status. There was – significantly – no mention of the much-talked-about East End Day-School and Kindergarten. But members of the Executive drew attention to the reconstruction plans of Stepney Borough Council: for it was now abundantly clear that neither the Borough nor the London County Council would allow the erection of more synagogues in the East End than were absolutely necessary to serve the needs of the *resident* Jewish population, which was known not to exceed 30,000 and to be in the throes of rapid contraction. Compensation would of course be forthcoming where synagogue premises were compulsorily purchased; but few of these synagogues would be rebuilt.

The Executive's adoption of this Memorandum, without dissent, signalled the triumph of realism over misplaced sentimentality in relation to East End affairs. Some money was made available for synagogue refurbishment (for example, Cannon Street Road, the Commercial Road Great Synagogue, Fieldgate Street, Ainsworth Road, Philpot Street Sphardish and Notting Hill). But we hear no more of organised East-End opposition to the building of constituent synagogues in the suburbs, or to the overall policy of amalgamations – though the pace of these remained painfully slow. At the General Council held on 25 June 1951 there was general if reluctant support for Julius Jung's view that "Most of our Synagogues [in the East End] are closed during the week and a large number find it extremely difficult to get a minyan, even on the Sabbath".

Underlying this change of attitude in the early 1950s was an awareness of severe financial constraint. By the end of 1950 the Federation had agreed in principle to advances totalling £28,000. But there were very few assets available to honour these promises, other than those accruing to the Burial Society. In May 1951 the Executive Committee agreed to the transfer of a further £5,000 from the funds of the Society to the Constituent Synagogues Establishment Fund. The constituent synagogues themselves continued to run at a deficit, but this was partly because central control of their budgets was not as tight as it could or should have been: it was only in the financial year 1952-53 that detailed scrutiny of these budgets by head office began to be undertaken. Meanwhile, grants continued to be made to a wide variety of charities, both in Britain and Israel. In 1951-52 the expenditure of the Federation increased by 26 per cent but its income grew by only 9 per cent, resulting in a bank overdraft of some £11,000.

It was inevitable, therefore, that at this time the emphasis should have been on encouraging the affiliation of existing congregations rather than on the establishment of new constituents. Since the major areas of suburban settlement were under strong United Synagogue influence, the Federation looked instead to smaller and more individualistic but nonetheless viable communities, such as Greenford & District (admitted to affiliated status August 1950), Loughton & District (formed by Federation members bombed out of Stepney and now living on the LCC's Debden Estate, and admitted as an affiliate in June 1952), and Finchley Central Synagogue (admitted to affiliated status September 1954). Where grants were made to affiliated synagogues for the purpose of building or improvement these were – almost without exception – conditional upon the properties being assigned to Federation trustees (for example, the Leytonstone & Wanstead and Springfield synagogues).

In January 1953 the virtual moratorium on the encouragement of new constituent synagogues was brought to an end, in a manner which was, in a short space of years, to give the Federation a role in the organisation of Jewish Day Schools. The impetus came from two distinct sources. The Clapton Synagogue embarked upon an ambitious development programme, central to which was the erection of a communal hall, youth centre and Talmud Torah classrooms; the synagogue's honorary officers applied for a loan of £10,000, in return for the granting of which the title deeds would be made over to the

Federation. The Federation itself was in no position to make a loan of this size, but the Executive agreed to withdraw funds invested by the Burial Society (amounting to almost two-thirds of the Society's cash assets) on condition not merely that the loan be repaid at the rate of £1,000 per annum, but that interest of 3.5% be paid in compensation for the interest lost on the Burial Society's investments so withdrawn. In January 1954, the Clapton Synagogue having agreed to apply for constituent status, the General Council approved these proposals.

Negotiations had meanwhile been proceeding with the Governors of the Hillel House School, which used the premises of the *Ohel Shem* synagogue, Willesden, and the Zionist Federation, which was now interesting itself in assuming the role of an educational body, and which had financial resources to apply for this purpose. The matter was a delicate one, because the Zionist Federation was not itself an Orthodox Jewish organisation (though many Orthodox Jews identified with and belonged to it). In 1956 the Executive agreed to advance the sum of £2,000 to the Hillel House School towards the erection of a purpose-built school building adjacent to the synagogue; the building would remain the property of the Federation of Synagogues, but the Zionist Federation would contribute approximately £1,500 per annum towards the running of the School, and would be represented henceforth on its governing body.

This arrangement did not meet with complete unanimity in Federation circles. But those who were most anxious to preserve the uncompromisingly Orthodox credentials of the Federation were reassured when, later in the year, it was agreed to fill the post of Principal Rabbi by the appointment to it of Rabbi Morris Swift, a former part-time Dayan of the London Beth Din and at that time Rabbi of the Young Israel Movement on the West Coast of the USA. Swift, then 49 years of age, was already well-known in Federation circles, for his first ministerial post after obtaining *semichot* from the yeshivot of Mir,

Grodno and Ponivez had been at the Federation synagogue at Shepherd's Bush, in 1932.

Swift's tenure of the post of Principal Rabbi lasted barely one year. Like many other talented Rabbonim, he used his position in the Federation as an avenue for still further advancement within Anglo-Jewry (in 1957 he became a full-time member of the London Beth Din). But he remained with the Federation long enough to be able to play a key role in its negotiations with the Zionist Federation over the establishment of a second Day School, attached to the Clapton Synagogue. The possibility of building such a school had been discussed locally in 1955. Discussions resumed in June 1956, when the Zionists agreed to contribute £10,000 towards the erection of a two-storied building which would itself form an extension to the newly-built communal premises and youth centre. As in Willesden, the Zionist Federation would be financially responsible for the school itself, and had agreed to give undertakings as to the acceptability of the school's curriculum from the orthodox point of view.

These undertakings failed to placate all sections of the Federation's Executive. In opposing the Clapton plan, Rabbi M. Frydman told the Executive (30 August 1956) that "they all want Jewish schools, but they [religious people] wondered why the Zionists were offering such generous co-operation ... He was afraid that the Zionists might stress less religious education and more the importance of kibbutzim and soldiers". Abraham Olivestone declared that "The Zionist Federation was known to be a non-religious body and consisting in part of Shomer Hatzair people who are known to be agnostics". Such views were of course sincerely held and passionately expressed, but they ignored the fact that thousands of Jewish children in London were attending non-Jewish schools. Although the Chief Rabbi was known to be unhappy with the prospect of allowing the proliferation of Zionist Federation schools, Lederman argued that to open a school in co-operation with the Zionists, and in a scheme which gave the local rabbi (H. Rashbass) and the Principal Rabbi complete authority in religious matters, was altogether preferable to standing idly by whilst Zionists opened schools on their own.

A potentially divisive situation was resolved by Morris Swift, who visited Clapton and presented to the Executive a measured statement, pointing out that at both Edgware and Leeds schools run by the Zionist Federation had been opened with the approval and co-operation of local religious leaders who were members of the Mizrachi movement. Swift categorically refused to accede to the wishes of those, within as well as beyond the Federation of Synagogues, who urged him to formally ban Zionist participation in Day Schools, and he personally took responsibility for the text books and religious character of the Clapton school. "The school", he declared, "shall be subsidised by the Zionist Federation. The building will remain the building of the Federation of Synagogues. Its religious character will be our responsibility. Let us therefore, all of us, put our weight behind it and cease discussing its failings." On 1 October 1956 the Clapton Jewish Day School opened for business. The fears of its critics proved unfounded.

The decision to appoint Swift to the office of Principal Rabbi ought itself to be seen as part of a policy of federal development that Lederman had instituted on assuming the Presidency. In March 1952 a special committee established by the Executive to investigate the Federation's central administration concluded that the burden then falling on Julius Jung was too great for one man to bear, especially in view of his role (in which the Federation encouraged him) as chairman of the Aliens Committee of the Board of Deputies. The position was a delicate one. In 1950 Jung, then 56 years of age, had completed 25 years' service as Federation Secretary. At a reception held in his honour at Stoke Newington Town Hall a galaxy of Anglo-Jewish notables, led by Dayan Abramsky, Chief Rabbi Brodie, and the President of the Deputies (the Rev Dr A. Cohen) had paid him glowing tributes.

But some elements within the Federation felt that the amount of time Jung devoted to other, entirely worthy activities, left insufficient time for his official

Federation duties. Lederman's special committee suggested that while Jung be left in charge of policy matters, routine administrative duties be placed in the hands of a new official. So the Executive agreed to create – for Jung – the office of Executive Director (July 1952), to which he was immediately appointed, and to choose a new Secretary; this position was filled by Simon Wilsack the following year. Wilsack terminated this employment in 1955, and Jung retired in 1959 (he died on 9 May 1975). The division in administration between routine matters and policy initiatives was no longer felt to be necessary. Accordingly, the post of Clerk to the Federation was created, and given to Michael Goldman (1929-2014), who had served under Jung and who came from a family with strong Federation connections in Hackney; as the Federation's chief secretarial officer Goldman was to preside over its entire administration until his retirement in 1989.

A third element in the reform of federal activities concerned the status and authority of the *Va'ad HaRabbonim* and the Federation rabbinate. The irritation of the rabbinate at the appointment of Kopul Rosen as Principal Rabbi was noted in the previous chapter. Rosen had hoped to carve out for the rabbinate a much higher profile in the activities both of the Federation and of London Jewry, not least in relation to the supervision of *kashrut*. This was not to be. The United Synagogue was determined not to permit any development which might impair the suzerainty of the Chief Rabbi and the London Beth Din – sentiments with which Aaron Wright and Jack Goldberg heartily concurred. Grants to the *Va'ad* continued to be made, principally by the Federation Burial Society, and it continued to occupy separate offices – originally at 19a Leman Street but later at 34 Settles Street, the former premises of the Settles Street synagogue.

When Morris Lederman assumed the Federation presidency the *Va'ad* consisted of eleven rabbis, and the grants made to it were, in truth, subsidies paid by headquarters to bolster inadequate levels of remuneration provided by the employing synagogues. Not all Federation rabbis were *Va'ad* members.

The rabbis themselves were men of great distinction and piety (for example, Aaron Singer of the Philpot Street Great Synagogue; H. M. Bendas of the New Road Synagogue and a teacher at the Etz Chaim Yeshiva; and J. Szpetman of the Nelson Street Sphardish Synagogue and later of the East London Amalgamated Synagogue), but they lacked the resources and, in some instances, the generational awareness to make anything other than a modest contribution to the solution of the wider problems that beset Jewish existence in post-war London. Younger rabbis who obtained Federation posts were soon enticed by more challenging and rewarding positions elsewhere: Pinchas Shebson, for example, appointed to the *Ohel Shem* in 1949, resigned barely two years later to go to Southend-on-Sea, where his sparkling talents and inspirational leadership were warmly received.

To some extent the reduced status and low morale of the Federation rabbinate were certainly financial in origin. In October 1955 the General Council agreed without dissent to a recommendation from the Honorary Officers and Executive Committee that contributions to the Burial Society be increased to one shilling per week, half of which was to be devoted to educational purposes, but not necessarily exclusively to the LBJRE. This enabled the Federation to devote some resources to the refurbishment of Talmud Torahs and to the support of yeshivot, as well as to the payment of teachers' salaries. In October 1957 the General Council voted, by the necessary two-thirds majority, to amend the Constitution in order to give the Executive borrowing powers. The following month, partly as a result of pressure from the Federation's bankers (the Federation's overdraft having by then reached £25,000), the Council (by 72 votes to 58) supported a further recommendation, that male members of Federation synagogues "be called upon to make a contribution of 6d per week towards the purposes of the Federation of Synagogues". It is right to add that, even though widows were deliberately excluded from the scope of this recommendation, and even though special exemptions were granted to those of modest means, the decision was not made without a great deal of controversy and even threats of legal action by some malcontents. The resolution itself was not mandatory – though the vast majority of Federation synagogues implemented it. By the end of 1958 the overdraft had been reduced by about £18,000.

The gradual improvement in the financial position of the Federation enabled more thought to be given to the re-organisation of the *Va'ad*. The filling of the office of Principal Rabbi was one result of these deliberations. In February 1956 the Executive discussed a proposal with radical implications: to abolish the *Va'ad* and to split the Federation rabbinate into two distinct parts. Rabbis and ministers of affiliated congregations would henceforth deal only with pastoral matters that fell within the purview of their own communities. The *Va'ad* itself would be superseded by a Rabbinical Authority, composed of the rabbis of constituent synagogues and (when appointed) the Principal Rabbi, together with Rabbi S. J. Rabinow (of the Stamford Hill Beth Hamedrash and a founder (1942) of the Yesodey Hatorah Schools) as Honorary President and Rabbi J. H. Cymerman (of the Philpot Street Sphardish Synagogue and now the newly-appointed Rav of the Burial Society). The dismantling of the *Va'ad* would – it was argued – result in a saving of about £500 per annum, mainly because some of its more senior members would not wish to assume the responsibilities now envisaged – namely dealing with "all religious problems affecting the Federation as a whole, the raising of the religious and educational standard of our community and all other major religious issues of a fundamental character".

What was envisaged, however, was not the establishment of a separate Beth Din. "It was envisaged [Lederman declared] that the Senior [i.e. Principal] Rabbi of the Federation would be sitting as a Dayan of the [London] Beth Din and that two or three Federation Rabbis would also be on a Panel at the Beth Din." In tracing the history of the Federation we have noted several occasions when Federation rabbis served on the Beth Din of the United Synagogue's Chief Rabbi – but always in their personal capacities. The plan now put to the Executive was altogether different: a permanent status for the most senior rabbis of the Federation, amounting to nothing less than an ecclesiastical fusion of the sort Samuel Montagu had wanted at the turn of the century and involving –clearly – Federation recognition of the Chief Rabbinate.

This remarkable proposal, which was to lead to an even more remarkable agreement four years later, must be traced to events surrounding Morris Lederman's election to the presidency of the Federation. It will be recalled that this election had taken place in June 1951. At that time, Lederman worked for the London Shechita Board, on which the Federation was represented as a Parent Body, but whose Ecclesiastical Authorities remained the United Synagogue's Chief Rabbi and the Haham of the Spanish & Portuguese Jews' Congregation of London. Shortly after his election Lederman was offered a senior supervisory position with the Board, but on condition that he first resign the Federation presidency. One of the Federation's Vice-Presidents, M. Cooper, told a shocked meeting of the Executive Committee (27 October 1952) that "the Chief Rabbi and the Haham [Rabbi Dr S. Gaon] had come to the unanimous conclusion and had ruled that Mr. Lederman could not be President of a parent body and must resign from his position if he wished to obtain a paid position with the Shechita Board".

It is difficult to find any logic or principle behind this ruling. At the time it was said that the principle merely mirrored that applying to local authorities: an employee cannot be a council member, lest the position – as a council member – be used for her or his own personal benefit. In that case, why had Lederman not been forced to resign other Federation positions earlier in his career? In Federation circles it seemed that the ruling had been made in a wholly capricious manner, in order to dictate to the Federation its choice of president and, at the same time, force the Federation to acknowledge the supremacy of the United Synagogue's Chief Rabbinate. Behind the ruling the influence of the United Synagogue was seen at work. Charles Gaventa, a member of the Federation's Executive (and brother of Harry Gaventa, President of the Shechita Board), told the Executive that he felt it "ought to fight the decision, because they [the Ecclesiastical Authorities] had not singled out every parent body, but only the Federation of Synagogues".

For Morris Lederman the immediate question was that of his livelihood. He resigned as President of the Federation and on 13 November 1952 Abraham Mann became Acting President. But opinion within wider Anglo-Jewish circles turned against the Ecclesiastical Authorities in this matter. In July 1953, and backed by the Executive and Council of the Federation, Lederman assumed the presidency once more. The minutes of the Executive record that "member after member rose to express their delight at the President's decision" (30 July 1953). The following May Lederman was able to tell his colleagues that a personal settlement between himself and the Shechita Board had been reached.

But the wider issues raised by this unhappy episode were not so easily disposed of. Chief amongst these was the refusal of the Shechita Board to include the Federation Rabbinate as one of its Ecclesiastical Authorities. This, in turn, touched upon the powers of veto given, by virtue of the Shechita Board's constitution, to the Chief Rabbi and the Haham; since the Chief Rabbi was in all but name the employee of the United Synagogue, these powers could be and (as the pressure put upon Lederman demonstrated) were being used to subordinate the Federation to the whims of the United Synagogue. The Federation had played no part in the election of Chief Rabbi Brodie, yet marriage-authorisation fees had still to be paid to his Office, and his authority in vital matters of shechita and kashrut had to be acknowledged.

The position of the Federation Rabbinate in relation to the Shechita Board had been raised by the Federation in 1951. Two years later the Federation proposed that Law 16 of the Shechita Board be amended so as to include the Va'ad among the Board's Ecclesiastical Authorities "on the same footing as that of the Chief Rabbi and the Haham". It was made clear that this request would only be granted if the Chief Rabbi and the Haham approved. Brodie's view was that the matter should not be considered until the Federation had appointed a new Principal Rabbi. On 23 February 1953 the General Council considered but neither endorsed nor rejected a proposal from the Executive that the Federation instruct its representatives not to participate further in Shechita Board activities. In the event, it was fortunate that this threatened withdrawal did not take place, because Federation representatives played a key role in helping resolve Lederman's personal difficulties with the Board.

While these difficulties were in train, the larger issue could not be pursued. There were, however, still wider considerations to be taken into account, for at this time a national agitation began with the object of prohibiting shechita altogether. In 1955 a Bill was brought forward in Parliament with just this object, but was not proceeded with because of the Dissolution and General Election; it was, however, reintroduced the following year, and was heavily defeated at the second-reading state, after a concerted lobbying campaign by Anglo-Jewry in which Federation synagogues played a full part. Clearly, however, the impact of this campaign would have been severely blunted had it become known in the media that the very legitimacy of the Board of Shechita was under attack from within the orthodox Jewish community. The Federation therefore stayed its hand, and meanwhile proceeded with the search for and appointment of a new Principal Rabbi.

Morris Swift's appointment to this position, coinciding as it did with the victory over the anti-shechita agitation, signalled the commencement of an intensive effort by the Federation to have its status on the Shechita Board fully recognised. The hope was entertained that, as a former Dayan, Swift's credentials as an Ecclesiastical Authority of the Board would be conceded without further ado. Chief Rabbi Brodie intimated that he was only prepared to consent to this if the Federation were to recognise *his* authority first. As an apparent (if rather insulting) concession, however, Brodie intimated that Swift, or his deputy, might take part in the supervision of the baking of *matzot* for Passover; an invitation was actually extended to Swift for this purpose, but was countermanded by the United Synagogue. On 24 January 1957 the

Executive of the Federation empowered the Honorary Officers to arrange for the purchase and importation of *matzot*, under the authority of the Principal Rabbi, and for their sale in competition with those manufactured and sold under the authority of the Chief Rabbinate.

The smell of schism was in the air once more. Shorn of the complexities surrounding shechita, the baking of *matzot*, and Morris Lederman's personal position, the issue was really very simple, and it was reiterated in the starkest possible terms by the then President of the United Synagogue (Ewen Montagu, Louis Montagu's second son), at a meeting between the Honorary Officers of the United Synagogue and the Federation in mid-March. At that meeting (Lederman subsequently reported to his Executive) Montagu had "declared in blunt terms that as long as he was President of the United Synagogue, there would only be one Religious Authority of the Ashkenazim in this country and that would be the Chief Rabbi and nobody else. Rabbi [Morris] Swift could attend the Board of Shechita only as a member of the London Beth Din and not on behalf of the Federation of Synagogues". For its part the Federation Rabbinate adopted an equally uncompromising position. On 12 March the Federation's Honorary Officers met rabbis Swift, J. H. Cymerman, M. Fisher, P. Braceiner and H. Rashbass. Swift declared that the Rabbinate "had come to the unanimous conclusion that they could only recognise the authority of the Principal Rabbi and that, according to religious law, they could recognise no Rav who had the power of veto". Rabbi Michael Fisher went further. According to Julius Jung's typescript note of the meeting:

> *Rabbi Fisher deemed the present time to be a very historical one for the Federation of Synagogues ... He personally could see no advantage in the Principal Rabbi sitting on the Beth Din. There were many Batei Dinim in England all recognised by the Chief Rabbi ... The Federation Rabbinate could and should act, as a proper Beth Din ... such establishment of a Federation Beth Din would involve no financial expenditure as would the profitless recognition of the Chief Rabbinate.*

Morris Swift did not go quite this far, and he suggested a possible compromise: he announced that though the Federation Rabbinate did indeed want autonomy in religious matters pertaining to the Federation, they might agree to co-operate on an enlarged Beth Din, upon which some of them would sit "as equal partners".

The threat to import *matzot*, coupled with the public knowledge that the formation of a separate Beth Din was now 'on the agenda', led the United Synagogue to offer a vague promise to give more urgent consideration to the matter of the status of the Federation's Principal Rabbi as one of the Shechita Board's Ecclesiastical Authorities. Then the Principal Rabbi resigned (to rejoin the United Synagogue's Beth Din, but now as a full-time Dayan) – an event that was used as an excuse for further delay. On 6 November 1957 the Federation's Executive resolved as follows:

> *That, notwithstanding the fact that the position of Principal Rabbi has become vacant, we request a change of Clause 16 of the Shechita Board and demand a Representative on behalf of the Rabbinate in the absence of a Principal Rabbi to represent the Rabbinate of the Federation of Synagogues to the Board of Shechita. This request for Rabbinical representation must be resolved even if it means withdrawing the Federation representatives from the Shechita Board.*

Early in 1958 serious discussions were resumed, both with the Shechita Board and with the Chief Rabbi. Later that year the hand of the Federation was strengthened by Lederman's election to the Executive of the Board of Deputies and as Vice-President of the Kashrus Commission. On 10 September 1958 representatives of the United Synagogue, the Federation, the Spanish & Portuguese Jews' Congregation and the Western Synagogue, met, under Israel Brodie's chairmanship, to consider a proposal that the Shechita Board's Ecclesiastical Authorities be enlarged to include the Principal Rabbi of the Federation or a rabbi nominated by the Federation "and approved by the Chief Rabbi". The Federation Rabbinate declared this wording unacceptable, as they considered it derogatory to their dignity. However, they were prepared to accept the words "after consultation with the Chief Rabbi". On 8 October 1958, the Executive of the Federation sanctioned the continuation of negotiations on this basis. But Ewen Montagu stood firm: the word "consultation" was too loose; the Chief Rabbi must have the power to veto a Federation nominee.

Apparently, therefore, matters had not progressed. On 14 May 1959 the Executive decided unanimously that no representatives from the Federation would be elected onto the Shechita Board. On 22 July, following fresh elections to the General Council and the Executive, Lederman outlined proposals for marriages performed in Federation synagogues to be authorised by the Federation Rabbinate, and no longer by the Chief Rabbi's Office; the authorisation fee would be halved, from four guineas to two. "It was intended", said Lederman, "to empower the Rabbinate ... to act with the full authority of a Beth Din to deal with Kiddushin [marriages], Gittin [divorces] ... Proselytisation etc". As evidence of its serious intentions the Executive agreed to establish a Rabbinate Sub-Committee and an Interim Shechita Advisory Committee, the task of the latter being to make recommendations "on the arrangements to be adopted for the commencement of shechita under the auspices of the Federation of Synagogues". On 25 August 1959, the Executive approved the establishment of "The Beth Din of the Federation of Synagogues", and consented to the appointment as Dayanim of rabbis M. Fisher, S. Gukovitzki and I. Rudnick; it was further agreed that Dayan Dr M. Krausz, of the Leeds Beth Din, also be invited to serve. At the same time the Executive approved the institution of a separate Federation shechita organisation.

Although the proceedings of the Honorary Officers and the Executive took place behind closed doors, news of them inevitably reached the Jewish press and the wider community. For obvious reasons Chief Rabbi Brodie did not wish a separate Beth Din and shechita facility to be established; but his desire to reach a compromise with the Federation was being blocked by the United Synagogue. The Honorary Officers of the Federation showed remarkable patience, for the Executive decisions of 25 August 1959 were not put to the General Council (which of course endorsed them) until 7 March 1960. Events thereafter moved with astonishing rapidity. At a special meeting of the Executive held on 9 June 1960 Lederman was able to announce that agreement had been reached to amend Law 16 of the Board of Shechita so that its Ecclesiastical Authorities would henceforth be defined as the Chief Rabbi, the Haham or other head of Sephardim and, "acting under the authority" of the Chief Rabbi, members of the London Beth Din and "Under the terms of the Agreement between the Rabbinate of the Federation of Synagogues and the Chief Rabbi relating to the acceptance of his authority in Shechita, the Principal Rabbi of the Federation of Synagogues or a member of its Rabbinate".

The Shechita Board intimated that it would approve the new Law and, on the basis of that assurance, Lederman told the General Council on 29 June 1960 that the Federation would return to the Board, and that the Executive had selected ten representatives to attend its meetings. But the rather awkward phraseology of the proposed amendment to Law 16 obscured two most important further developments.

The "Agreement between the Rabbinate of the Federation of Synagogues and the Chief Rabbi relating to the acceptance of his authority in Shechita" (signed by Brodie, Lederman and Rabbi Cymerman on behalf of the Federation Rabbinate on 13 June 1960) provided for the representation of the Federation Rabbinate not merely on the Board of Shechita but also on the Kashrus Commission, the LBJRE and on the list of signatories sanctioning *matzot* and other Passover products; when Federation rabbis acted as rabbinical supervisors for the Shechita Board they would be paid by the Board, not the Federation. Later that year Dayan Krausz was nominated as the Federation representative on the Ecclesiastical Authorities of the Board, while the Kashrus Commission confirmed the appointment of rabbis M. Fisher and S. Gukovitzki as Federation members of its Ecclesiastical Authorities.

Moreover, the Chief Rabbi had, in the agreement, explicitly recognised the Federation Rabbinate as an independent rabbinical authority for members and synagogues of the Federation; whenever Federation synagogues or members took a dispute to the London Beth Din, a member of the Federation Rabbinate was to be asked to act as one of the Dayanim. In return, and as stated in the agreement, the Federation Rabbinate undertook to accept the authority of the Chief Rabbi and not to constitute itself as a separate Beth Din.

The agreement of 1960 was not quite what the Executive of the Federation had had in mind in 1956: a permanent status for members of the Federation Rabbinate upon the London Beth Din. But it clearly represented a major step in that direction and could well have led to closer co-operation between the Federation and the United Synagogue, the principal paymaster of both the Beth Din and the Chief Rabbinate. In accepting the overarching authority of the Chief Rabbi the Federation demonstrated the utter sincerity of its desire not to be the cause of further splits in the Orthodox Jewish community of London. Had those who led the United Synagogue shown a similar degree of statesmanship and compromise in the wider interest, the two synagogal bodies might have moved closer together. But this was not to be.

An examination of the motives of those who led the United Synagogue at that time is, strictly speaking, no part of the objects of the present work. Curiously, the events outlined above do not appear in Dr Aubrey Newman's centenary history of the United Synagogue. Still more curious is the fact that, in a letter written to Morris Lederman on 10 May 1966, Sir Isaac Wolfson (who had in 1962 succeeded Ewen Montagu as President of the United Synagogue) denied having had any knowledge of the agreement of 13 June 1960 prior to a meeting with Lederman on 28 April 1966 – even though one of the witnesses to the 1960 agreement had been Asher Wingate, a Treasurer of the United Synagogue, and even though the post of Secretary to the United Synagogue throughout this period was held by just one person, Alfred Silverman.

We can, however, be much less uncertain about the motives of the Federation of Synagogues in consenting to the agreement of 1960. Foremost among these was a keen desire to preserve the form and fabric of the Federation in a period of obvious and undeniable transformation, the major feature of which was the reduction in the number of East End affiliated synagogues. By a process of persuasion that was both heavily time-consuming and often frustrating, Julius Jung and successive Honorary Officers were able to obtain some movement towards a reduction in the number of East End congregations. It was (Lederman confessed to the Executive, 5 May 1954) regrettable "that the full spirit of co-operation was not always evident on the part of the Honorary Officers of some Synagogues". To the General Council on 13 September 1954 Lederman was a good deal blunter: "I must tell you that not only have I not received the co-operation I thought I had a right to expect, but I have met unreasonable opposition which endangers the future of our children and our Community."

One amalgamation that was achieved relatively painlessly was that of the Croydon and Addiscombe synagogues, in 1954. But in relation to the East End, war-damage and compulsory-purchase moneys were often used to reconstruct synagogues for which there was – or was evidently soon likely to be – no need. One example of this was the Mile End New Town synagogue, rebuilt and reconsecrated in 1954; another was the New Road synagogue, partially reconstructed and completely renovated the following year. At the General Council of 3 October 1955 Lederman appealed publicly to the Honorary Officers and Board of Management of the Stepney Orthodox synagogue, who were persisting in their determination to rebuild, whereas the Executive of the Federation would have much rather have had this community amalgamate with the Jubilee Street synagogue. In the event, both these synagogues were completely rebuilt, though they were but a very short distance from each other, a fact which triggered a public condemnation by Rabbi Frydman at the General Council of 9 September 1957.

Although the Federation had no legal authority to prevent such actions, there were other weapons at its disposal. Often, compensation from the public purse still fell short of the finance required by ambitious East End managements. When the members of the Bethnal Green synagogue decided to rebuild their place of worship, the war-damage settlement amounted to only £28,000, whereas the rebuilding cost (based on the plans favoured by local stalwarts) was nearer £45,000. Bethnal Green therefore applied to the Federation (November 1955) for a loan of £15,000, in order to finance the construction of a building that would accommodate 350 men and 100 women, and which would include flats for a Rabbi and a Chazan. The Executive (and in due course the General Council) agreed, but only on condition that Bethnal Green apply for constituent status.

On 30 April 1956 the General Council somewhat intemperately referred back a recommendation from the Finance Sub-Committee that any loan exceeding £3,000 be conditional in future on opting for constituent status. But although it could not be enforced as a general rule, that policy was in fact closely adhered to – and not only in relation to the East End. To assist the much-needed complete rebuilding of the Woolwich & Plumstead synagogue a loan of £12,500 was agreed, provided the community opted for constituent status (approved by the General Council in September 1957). The Greenford & District synagogue was granted a loan of £1,000 towards buying a new site, but subject to the stipulation that the land be purchased in the name of the Trustees of the Federation. The same condition was attached in respect of a loan to the Finchley Central Synagogue.

An incident in 1956 illustrated the dangers in permitting East End congregations to go their own way. The Limehouse synagogue (which had been destroyed and never rebuilt) and its Talmud Torah had been partially repaired, apparently without the prior consent or knowledge of the trustees; but a dispute with the builders had resulted in the possibility that the Talmud Torah, together with the *Sifrei Torah* and synagogue silver, might have to be sold to pay for the legal and building expenses. The Federation had to step in at short notice to prevent this catastrophe from taking place. The General Council was evidently not of a mind to force synagogues to opt for constituent status. But as the active memberships of redundant East End synagogues contracted, so the balance of opinion on the General Council, and within the Boards of Management of those synagogues which were still viable, became less hostile to a greater measure of federal direction.

In this regard, the agreement of the Bethnal Green Great Synagogue to apply for constituent status (granted September 1957) was a straw in the wind. In November 1957 the Commercial Road Great Synagogue successfully made a similar application, but with the vital difference that, in so doing, it was not also asking for a loan. The reason for the application was, quite simply, that by becoming a constituent the Commercial Road congregation would enjoy the benefit of head-office guidance and advice and, more importantly, would share with the Federation its financial responsibilities: instead of fighting the constituent synagogues of the suburbs, East End congregations were now deciding to join them. Constituent status was, in short, becoming fashionable. In 1958 the Croydon & District and Gladstone Park & Neasden synagogues were admitted as constituents, as was the *Sinai* Synagogue (Golders Green) early the following year.

At this time, too, the number and frequency of East End amalgamations increased. Lederman was able to announce to the General Council on 17 February 1959 the merger of the Philip Street & Shadwell Synagogue with the Commercial Road Great; the Mile End & Bow with the Stepney Orthodox; the Rosener with the Agudath Achim; and the Chevrah Torah with the Bethnal Green Great. The proceeds of the sale of the Shadwell property were hoped by some to be earmarked for the erection of a Jewish Day School on the site of the Philpot Street Amalgamated Synagogue; but it was quickly realised that the need simply did not exist. In January 1959 Mr A. E. Magen had confessed to the Executive that "attendances at the Commercial Road Talmud Torah had dropped from 400 to 80, and a recent canvassing campaign ... had resulted in only three promises to attend. He therefore doubted whether the proposed Day School would attract many children". In 1960 the Commercial Road Great and the Philpot Street Amalgamated made further absorptions of more or less redundant nearby congregations. In April 1961 the Ilford Federation Synagogue was admitted to constituent status, and property was purchased in Coventry Road, Ilford, on which to build a new house of worship, Talmud Torah and communal hall. The following year the Great Garden Street Synagogue (Whitechapel) also became a constituent.

The very nature of the Federation was therefore changing. Although there were still roughly twice as many members in the affiliated as in the constituent synagogues, and although most of these affiliated congregations were still to be found in the East End, their memberships were increasingly located in the suburbs. To this extent there was some truth in the accusation that the Federation was – or at least was in danger of becoming – a mere burial society. The fate of the Hendon Federation Synagogue illustrates the difficulties caused by this trend. In 1960, realising that many Federation members resided in the Hendon area of north-west London but were obliged to attend synagogues of the United Synagogue or of the Union of Orthodox Hebrew Congregations, the Honorary Officers of the Federation obtained the approval of the Executive to proceed with the purchase of a site in Hendon on which to build a Federation house of worship. A Hendon Federation Synagogue was, accordingly, established, on paper, and a few members were recruited to it. But the Federation did not possess the necessary funds to implement the scheme by itself, and negotiations with other bodies, to share the use of jointly-owned buildings (for example, to rebuild the Machzike Hadass in Hendon as a Federation constituent, and to appoint the Principal Rabbi as its Rav) never bore fruit. The scheme was quietly dropped. It was to remain many years before Hendon, encompassing one of the largest concentrations of Jews in Great Britain, was to have a Federation presence.

There was indeed some growth within the Federation in the 1950s, especially at Ilford (where male membership in 1960 stood at 340) and at Edgware (where an extension to the *Yeshurun* synagogue was authorised by the General Council in 1961). By the end of the 1950s the financial position of the Federation had improved sufficiently to permit the implementation of significant building programmes. There were other Federation centres which, though not operating on the scale of Edgware and Ilford, were nonetheless flourishing and expanding: Croydon & Putney, Clapton, Springfield, Tottenham and West Hackney most prominently among them. Grants were still being made to a very wide range of Jewish causes, both in the United

Early edition of Hamaor, 1962

Kingdom and Israel. In April 1961, the General Council approved the principle of a Federation "News Bulletin". Although *Hamaor* ("The Light"), which first appeared that month, was not quite in this mould (*Hamaor* was at that time largely devoted to articles on Orthodoxy and Rabbonim of old), its appearance – and survival – attested to the vitality of the Federation as a body of interested and articulate Jewish men and women.

But all this activity was taking place within an overall and undeniable contraction. In spite of valiant efforts by some East End enthusiasts, the spectre of an elderly and decaying Jewish community in the East End was already clearly visible. In December 1961 Lederman told the Executive "that he understood the attitude of East End Synagogues but it was obvious that there were far too many than were needed to cater for the Jewish community in the area. Large sums of money could be saved if these synagogues would amalgamate to form four or five synagogues in the East End which was the most that was required". On 30 January 1963 the General Council could do no other than endorse his view that the plan for an East London Jewish Day School be abandoned. Later that year, with the approval of the General Council, the latest version of the grandiose scheme to spend £100,000 on an East London Jewish Communal Centre was finally laid to rest.

The Clapton Jewish Day School was flourishing – for the moment – but in an area where the Jewish community had ceased to grow, and out of which Jews were beginning even now to move. Most constituent synagogues operated at a deficit; surpluses, where they existed, were exceedingly small. The *Shomrei Hadath* posed a particular problem. The small community there was in decline and the building itself was in a bad state of repair. The Honorary Officers of the Federation wished to sell what was after all Federation property, but the Executive was unwilling to override the wishes of local synagogue members. Income from the burial of non-members (in times past a fruitful source of extra revenue) was now declining. But so too was income from the Burial Society, which fell from £47,896 in 1960 to £45,215 in 1962. Some members of the Federation's Executive blamed this on the 1959 decision of the United Synagogue to allow members of the Federation (and other burial societies) to transfer to the United Synagogue Burial Society with immediate benefit rights. This may well have been the case, but whether it was or not the Federation was in 1963 obliged to increase its own membership subscription by sixpence a week.

The overall financial position of the Federation was at this time appreciably stronger than it had been a decade earlier. True, the Building Fund was (1963) overdrawn to the extent of some £37,000; but this overdraft was more than covered by land and buildings which the Federation itself now owned. It was absurd to say (as some had said in the mid-1950s) that the Federation was on the verge of bankruptcy. It wasn't. Yet it was equally absurd to believe that the Federation in the 1960s could emulate the Federation of the 1930s. At that time it had indeed been the largest Jewish communal organisation in London. This pre-eminence had been lost.

In public the Federation was understandably reticent about its membership position. But we know from the returns made by individual Federation synagogues to the Board of Deputies (returns which included members of such synagogues who were not Burial Society members) that in 1964 the total membership of the Federation (males plus females who were members in their own right) was approximately 16,000, whereas that of the United Synagogue was about 36,000. Little wonder, therefore, that at the General Council on 31 July 1963 one representative should actually have suggested that "a Working Committee be established to discuss with the United Synagogue ways and means of integrating the work of the two bodies". The suggestion was not taken up. Yet the question which had surely prompted it remained: was there any independent future for the Federation of Synagogues, or did its destiny lie in an absorption within what was now the largest Ashkenazi community in the metropolis?

In consenting, as part of the Shechita Board agreement of 1960, to recognise the authority of the United Synagogue's Chief Rabbi, the lay and ecclesiastical leaderships of the Federation had held out to the United Synagogue an olive branch. Further evidence of their good intentions was provided during the great controversy of 1962 over the Principalship of Jews' College, which it was made clear would not (contrary to previous expectation) be offered to Rabbi Dr. Louis Jacobs, whose theology had come under suspicion. Lederman told the Executive (13 February 1962) that the Federation "would support the Chief Rabbi on this issue if he took a firm stand". And so it was. In 1963 the General Council agreed to an annual grant to the College of £600, in return for which two Federation representatives were to sit on its Council while its Examination Board was to include a member of the Federation Rabbinate.

In 1964 two opportunities presented themselves which might have been used to facilitate a still closer relationship between the United Synagogue and the Federation.

The first arose out of Chief Rabbi Brodie's desire to amend the constitution of the Kashrus Commission, which at that time was organised on a synagogal basis. Brodie wished it to function as an executive composed of fifteen representatives of the United Synagogue, eight of the Federation and three of the London Beth Din. As one of the parent bodies, and following the agreement of 1960, the Federation had a right to expect that its Rabbinate would be included in the Commission's Ecclesiastical Authorities. To this the United Synagogue would not consent. In the absence of any agreement, the biennial elections to the Kashrus Commission were held as usual but, contrary to past experience and (in Lederman's view) "owing to certain irresponsible manoeuvres" (namely a letter sent on United Synagogue notepaper on 25 September 1964 soliciting votes for United Synagogue representatives), not one Federation candidate was elected either to the executive of the Commission or as one of its honorary officers. Effectively, therefore, the Federation now had no voice whatsoever in the Commission's administration.

The posture adopted by the United Synagogue seemed to be that it was – certainly in London – the prime custodian of Orthodox Judaism. Reminding a special meeting of the Federation's Executive and Kashrus Commission delegates held on 20 October 1964 of the precise terms of the 1960 agreement, Lederman declared that

> None of the decisions in the Agreement had been adhered to. Whenever Rabbi Cymerman had raised the matter with the Chief Rabbi he had urged him to be patient ... representations had been made to the Federation to support Jews' College ... yet the Federation's representatives on the Jews' College Council had not been elected to serve on any of the Sub-Committees. From this and similar incidents it was clear that there was an element amongst the Honorary Officers of the United Synagogue who were determined to undermine the Federation of Synagogues. Perhaps this was, in fact, the policy of the United Synagogue – he could not say. Some time previously the United Synagogue had sent some eight or nine thousand registered letters to their members who were also members of the Federation, asking them to relinquish their membership of the Federation.

There was no doubt that the Federation had been slapped in the face. It was about to be kicked in the stomach.

The abortive negotiations concerning the Kashrus Commission had been overtaken by the need, in view of Israel Brodie's imminent retirement, to discuss the future of the Chief Rabbinate. In the summer of 1964 the Federation had indicated its willingness to participate in the election of a new Chief Rabbi, and to recognise the new Chief Rabbi as titular head of the Federation Rabbinate (thus explicitly abolishing the office of Principal Rabbi of the Federation), provided that religious administration in Greater

London was shared by the United Synagogue's Beth Din and the Federation Rabbinate working under the Chief Rabbi's chairmanship. Significantly, the Federation did not fuss over its proposed representation at the Chief Rabbinate Conference: 10 representatives (as had been offered in 1948), as against 12 for the provincial communities and 25 (an increase of 10) for the United Synagogue. The Honorary Officers of the United Synagogue made an interesting and attractive counter-proposal: that the United Synagogue's Beth Bin be reorganised to include the Federation Rabbinate.

The idea was not, of course, new. The hope that it might now be realised was, however, materially improved as a result of a written "Heads of Agreement" approved by Messrs Alfred Woolf, Mark Kleiner and Reuben Kandler on behalf of the United Synagogue and Morris Lederman, Elchanan Chanan and Abraham Olivestone on behalf of the Federation. The Agreement was dated 26 February 1965. By its terms, following the appointment of a new Chief Rabbi, four members of the Federation Rabbinate were to join the London Beth Din, over whom the Chief Rabbi would continue to preside as "Av Beth Din". The Federation Rabbinate and the office of Principal Rabbi would then cease to exist, but the Va'ad would remain, under the presidency of the Chief Rabbi, "to deal with the domestic religious affairs of the Federation of Synagogues". No new appointments of Federation-nominated Dayanim would be made without the prior approval of the Chief Rabbi, but the Federation would be free not to accept a decision of the Chief Rabbi were it to differ from that of the enlarged Beth Din. The financial responsibilities of the Federation would extend no further than providing for the salaries and pension arrangements of the Dayanim it nominated.

This agreement could have provided a solid basis for a much closer and more harmonious relationship between the Federation and the United Synagogue. On the understanding of its having been approved by both sides, the Federation participated in the election of Israel Brodie's successor. Morris Lederman was elected to the Council of the United Synagogue and was a member of the delegation which travelled to Israel to invite Rabbi Dr Jacob Herzog to accept the post of Chief Rabbi. A detailed scheme of reform of the Kashrus Commission was agreed to, guaranteeing that a vice-presidency and a treasurership would go to Federation nominees, and reserving to the Federation three places on the Commission's executive.

For a moment, therefore, in the summer of 1965, it seemed that an entirely new chapter in the history of London Jewry was about to be written. Then the entire fabric of the Agreement fell apart. Dr Herzog became ill, and was unable to accept the post of Chief Rabbi. The Honorary Officers of the United Synagogue appear to have used this as an excuse to delay placing before their own Executive Council the February 1965 Heads of Agreement for ratification; their view was that ratification (which Lederman and his colleagues had been led to expect would take place in November 1965) should now wait until after the election of a new Chief Rabbi. Their underlying motives must remain a matter for conjecture. In a letter written by Lederman Sir Isaac Wolfson on 4 May 1966 the Federation President recalled that when they had met on 28 April "You mentioned that some of the Honorary Officers of the United Synagogue felt that I am difficult to deal with, that I cannot be relied upon to honour mutual decisions". But in view of the fact that the Heads of Agreement had been approved by both sides, this excuse fails to convince. We know that in his reply (10 May 1966) Wolfson admitted that he would not have been a party to the meeting of 28 April had he known of the existence of the Shechita agreement of 1960. In Federation circles it was widely believed that the United Synagogue had only entered into the 1965 Heads of Agreement in order to be assured of financial support (which would have amounted to £2,750 per annum) from the Federation for the Chief Rabbinate. That may well have been so but, in that case, why jeopardise this support by refusing to proceed with ratification?

The most likely explanation is also (and usually) the simplest. The policy of those who led the United Synagogue at that time had indeed changed early in

1965, but without much enthusiasm, and Dr Herzog's ill-health provided an opportunity to revert to the former view: that the Federation of Synagogues was best killed off by attrition, not kindness. Perhaps there were some in the United Synagogue who doubted that the Federation would ever dare to establish its own Beth Din or authorise its own Kashrut. These steps had, after all, been much talked about but never yet implemented. If that was indeed the private view of Isaac Wolfson and his colleagues, they had made a grave miscalculation.

The Federation did not participate in the resumed Chief Rabbinate Conference (20 February 1966) and has never recognised the authority of Brodie's successors (rabbis Jakobovits, Sacks and Mirvis). On 14 April 1966 the General Council of the Federation approved (with only three dissentients) recommendations from the Honorary Officers and Executive to establish a Beth Din of the Federation of Synagogues. Four Dayanim (Rabbis Krausz, Fisher, Rudnick and S. Gukovitzki) were at once appointed, with the Rev I. M. Braier as Clerk, and commenced issuing licences for marriages in Federation synagogues and dealing with other matters (for example the conversion of an adopted child) which are within the normal purview of Orthodox Batei Din. As a responsible Orthodox body, and in line with the practice of, for example, the Union of Orthodox Hebrew Congregations, the Federation agreed at once to provide the Marriage Authorisation Office of the United Synagogue's Chief Rabbi with a record of marriages authorised by the Federation Beth Din – but only after such authorisation had been granted – in order to maintain the integrity of one central record for British Jewry.

In establishing its own Beth Din the Federation had at last become a *kehilla* - a self-governing community – in its own right.

CHAPTER SIX

Contraction, Crisis and Rebirth

The momentous step which the Federation took in 1966 in establishing its own Beth Din was quickly followed by others, intended not merely to give the Federation a distinctive and separate character, but to allow it much more control over its own resources. At the same meeting of the General Council at which the decision to form a separate Beth Din was taken, it was also decided to sever all connections between the Federation and the LBJRE. This decision, too, had an extensive pre-history, to which some reference must now be made.

We have already noted that the LBJRE had been set up in 1945 with the enthusiastic support of the then Federation leadership. The LBJRE was primarily responsible for the salaries of teachers; accommodation, lighting and heating were the responsibility of the local education committees of the

LBJRE's parent bodies. Jack Goldberg, who in 1948 was elected a Treasurer of the LBJRE, was assiduous in his efforts to persuade all Federation synagogues to pay the Education Tax; and most did so. In 1957 Morris Lederman added his authority to that of Chief Rabbi Brodie and United Synagogue president Ewen Montagu in persuading the Kashrus Commission to amend its constitution in order to enable it to charge a small fee to its licence-holders in order to boost LBJRE revenue.

By the mid-1960s the bulk of the LBJRE's income came from the United Synagogue. But this was as it should have been. In 1964 about 7,806 children attended United Synagogue centres, while 1,231 attended centres maintained by the Federation; in addition, some 2,000 children attended withdrawal classes run by the LBJRE in non-Jewish day schools. There was, therefore, a just correlation between the £100,000 contribution made by the United Synagogue to the finances of the LBJRE in 1965, as against the Federation's £18,000 and the £2,500 contributed by some independent congregations.

Some years previously the LBJRE had embarked upon a policy of "regionalisation" for its senior classes (for pupils over the age of eleven); in each area of London these classes were grouped in one set of premises, invariably under United Synagogue control. Rightly or wrongly, Lederman accused the United Synagogue of exploiting these arrangements in order to induce parents who were Federation members to switch their membership to the United Synagogue. Addressing the General Council in April 1966 Lederman charged that the LBJRE had "strongly resisted the ... recognition of centres ... attached to new Federation Synagogues". A number of incidents appear to have brought matters to a head: the refusal of the LBJRE to recognise the classes attached to the *Sinai* Synagogue; the impact of regionalisation on the Federation classes at Neasden and Ilford; above all, the decision to establish the Finchley centre at the Kinloss Gardens premises of the United Synagogue, and not at the Federation premises at Finchley Central.

The chairman of the LBJRE at that time was the peppery Salmond Levin, a Vice-President of the United Synagogue. The leadership of the Federation alleged that the closure of and discrimination against Federation centres by the LBJRE was part of the war of attrition against the Federation itself. Lederman asked "What business has the Board [LBJRE] to close Federation centres without consulting the Federation ... Is he [Levin] using his office in the Board to ... diminish the strength and influence of the Federation as a synagogal body by closing our centres and taking our children away by means of regionalisation schemes? ... Centres which refused to enter the regionalisation scheme were forced to submit by the threat that teachers would be withdrawn. Is this responsible management? It is more like blackmail". The General Council was minded to agree with this interpretation, and therefore resolved to approve recommendations from the Honorary Officers and Executive to establish an independent education authority – the London Talmud Torah Council – to run Federation Talmud Torahs and Hebrew Classes. The Council, with Rabbi Frydman and subsequently Abraham Olivestone as its chairman, commenced functioning on 1 June 1966, supervising the work of 18 centres with an initial roll of over 900 pupils. Some months later Rabbi L. Spector was appointed as its Education Officer.

The establishment of a separate Beth Din also had important consequences in the field of *kashrut* supervision. The Federation had withdrawn from the Kashrus Commission in 1964, so that the Commission was now virtually a sub-committee of the United Synagogue. But membership of the London Board for Shechita continued as before and of course the Federation retained its statutory representation on the Rabbinical Commission for the Licensing of Shochetim. In 1966 the Federation Beth Din began issuing its own *kashrut* licences. At the same time the Federation strengthened its position in relation to the Shechita Board by appointing a new Principal Rabbi, who it was hoped would (following the agreement of 1960) become one of the Board's Ecclesiastical Authorities.

The appointment – now styled the *Rav Rashi* - was given to Rabbi Dr E. W. Kirzner, a native of Lithuania who at that time held a position in New York, but who had for fourteen years (1926-40) been Rav of the Stamford Hill Beth Hamedrash. On 31 October 1966 Kirzner met members of the Federation's Executive and assured them that Rabbi Dr Immanuel Jakobovits, the Chief Rabbi-elect of the United Synagogue but then also in New York, "was a man who wanted peace in the community". On 7 March 1967 Lederman was able to report to the Executive that Kirzner and Jakobovits had met in New York and had agreed what was termed a "document of understanding". In this document (dated 25 January) the United Synagogue's Chief Rabbi was recognised as the "spokesman and authority" of the Ashkenazi communities within British Jewry, but he for his part agreed to consult with the *Rav Rashi* of the Federation on all policy decisions and public statements affecting the Federation. Kirzner and Jakobovits also agreed to give "full and unqualified" recognition to each other's rabbinical rulings, and they declared themselves in favour of a unified Beth Din (encompassing also the Spanish & Portuguese community) and of the joint administration of shechita and *kashrut*; they also looked forward "to the eventual representation of the Federation of Synagogues on the Chief Rabbinate Council".

As a result of this understanding the Federation was assured that Kirzner would be recognised as an Ecclesiastical Authority of the Shechita Board. Moves were made to enable the Federation to rejoin the Kashrus Commission. Perhaps also as a result, the Office of the Chief Rabbi acquiesced in the recognition of marriages authorised by the Beth Din of the Federation: this amounted, in effect, to recognition of the authority of the Beth Din.

On 17 February 1967 the *Jewish Chronicle* published an interview between its New York correspondent and rabbis Kirzner and Jakobovits. Rabbi Jakobovits, who had already been privately chastised by the United Synagogue's Dayanim (see M. Persoff, *Hats in the Ring* (2013), pp. 202-3) was adamant that the agreement he and Kirzner they had reached in New York was "a purely rabbinical understanding between the two of us and is not binding on, or involving, any other parties". The fact was that however amicable might have been this "rabbinical understanding", it did not have the support of the United Synagogue's ecclesiastical or lay leaderships, who had not been parties to it, and whose policy of unremitting antagonism towards the Federation risked being compromised by it. Privately, to the United Synagogue's Secretary, Alfred Silverman, Jakobovits had in any case offered the view that "Once things are quiet, the Federation will resume its relative impotence and insignificance in the community at large as before, whatever formal concessions are made to them." (Persoff, pp.201-2). As Dr Persoff concludes, "The Jakobovits-Kirzner 'understanding' began to unravel within months of its signing," (Persoff, p. 219). By the summer of 1968 it seemed clear that the most that was going to be conceded was an invitation to Kirzner to join the Ecclesiastical Authorities of the Shechita Board in his personal capacity.

In relation to the Kashrus Commission the United Synagogue was in an even stronger position, for its Beth Din had the power of veto in relation to any matter affecting the Commission's constitution, and the Dayanim of the Court of the Chief Rabbi were reportedly adamant that they were not prepared to share this authority with anyone, no matter how eminent a Talmudist he might be. But towards the end of 1968, and faced with the possibility that the Federation, having carried out its long-stated intention to establish a separate Beth Din, would indeed set up an independent shechita authority, Law 16 of the Shechita Board was at long last amended to give the *Rav Rashi* of the Federation – but not his deputy – a position as an Ecclesiastical Authority of the Board, of which Abraham Olivestone was subsequently elected Vice-President.

For a time the issue of Federation participation in the work of the Shechita Board therefore subsided, while the Federation's own Kashrus Board continued to expand its activities, under Rabbi Frydman's chairmanship. In November 1968 Kirzner's appointment was, by mutual consent, terminated, reportedly on the grounds of his ill-health. Dayan Fisher, then 52 years of age, became Acting (and later full) *Rav Rashi* and, after some hesitation, the Shechita Board recognised him as representing the Federation among its Ecclesiastical Authorities. The death of Rabbi H. J. Cymerman and the retirement of Dr Krausz (who died in 1971) had created vacancies on the Federation's Beth Din, to which Rabbi P. Braceiner, of the Finchley Central Synagogue, was now (1970) appointed.

The resignation of Dr Kirzner led to the resurrection and further discussion of the perennial and much-discussed plan to merge the post of Principal Rabbi within that of the Chief Rabbi of the United Synagogue. But these discussions, which had by March 1971 resulted in an exchange of memoranda with Dr Jakobovits, were overtaken by two separate developments.

The first involved the great crisis of 1970-71 at the Board of Deputies of British Jews. This arose out of the determination of non-Orthodox elements among the Deputies to amend Clause 43 of the Board's constitution so as to confer consultative status upon the religious leaderships of those congregations not under the jurisdiction either of the United Synagogue's Chief Rabbi or of the Haham of the Spanish & Portuguese Jews' Congregation. The Federation of Synagogues, along with the Union of Orthodox Hebrew Congregations and some sections of the United Synagogue, opposed this stratagem, and Messrs Lederman and Olivestone became members of the "ad hoc Orthodox committee" formed in August 1970 to defend – ironically – the authority of the Chief Rabbi even if this meant putting aside, in the overriding interests of Orthodoxy, the claims of the Beth Din of the Federation, or of its Principal Rabbi, to be an Ecclesiastical Authority of the Deputies. Initially Olivestone and Lederman believed they enjoyed the unflinching support of Jakobovits in this matter, for he had indicated to them the possibility that some or all of the religious functions of the Board of Deputies might have to be phased out if no agreement could be reached; indeed on 24 August 1971 he assured Bernard Homa that "The Haham and I ... are determined to maintain [the principle that] ... the Board's constitution must not accord any religious recognition to Progressive Judaism and its spiritual leaders".

In the event – as is well known – Jakobovits did acquiesce in the amendment of Clause 43 (24 October 1971). Members of the ad hoc committee felt that they had been betrayed. On 15 November 1971 the Beth Din of the Federation issued a *P'sak Din* to the effect that the amended Clause 43 was contrary to *Halacha*, and advising that the Federation withdraw from the Board of Deputies, which it did. Subsequently, relying on the inclusion in the Board's *Annual Report* for 1971-72 of the view of the Board's Executive Committee, that the Board "must continue to follow any interpretation of Halacha as given by the Ecclesiastical Authorities", and relying also upon a legal opinion that the Deputies, having approved the *Annual Report*, were bound by the interpretation enshrined therein, the Federation's Beth Din rescinded the *P'sak* to permit the Federation to return to the Deputies (29 April 1973) in order to have Clause 43 further amended, along the lines adumbrated in the *Annual Report*, at "the first opportunity".

This additional amendment has never taken place. But Federation Deputies continued to act as champions of Orthodox opinion, and in a further conflict at the Board, in 1984, over attempts to stifle the Orthodox viewpoint in official representations made by the Deputies to governmental bodies, the Federation presence proved a powerful antidote to the less robust sections of the United Synagogue. In its immediate context, however, the crisis of 1970-71 soured relations between Jakobovits and the Federation, and undoubtedly made the leadership of the Federation less enthusiastic than it might otherwise have been about elevating him to the office of Principal Rabbi.

But it was not only with Jakobovits personally that relations deteriorated at this time. Angered by the boldness of the Federation in establishing its own Kashrus Board, the United Synagogue announced (1970) that only caterers licensed by the Kashrus Commission would henceforth be permitted to operate on United Synagogue premises. In July 1972 Lederman informed the

Federation's Executive that an imaginative solution to the problem, involving a system of joint licensing of caterers, had had to be abandoned because of opposition from the Chief Rabbi's Beth Din. One member of the Executive revealed

> *That it was the London Beth Din which had prevented through its veto the merger of the Kashrus Commission and the London Board of Shechita and other kashrus authorities unless they remained the sole Ecclesiastical Authorities of the new body. The London Beth Din were apparently determined to exclude from general communal administration the religious authorities of the other Orthodox institutions. The Shechita Board had been informed that if the Board, the Federation Kashrus Board, the Kashrus Commission and the Spanish and Portuguese Congregation's Kashrus Authority all signified their support of [sic] the proposed merger in writing, the United Synagogue would take steps to effect the proposal. The required signatures had, in fact, been obtained and the United Synagogue had accordingly required the [Chief Rabbi's] Beth Din to withdraw its veto. But the Beth Din had adamantly refused.*

Another proof of the hostility of the Chief Rabbis' Office to the Federation was provided by the absence of any reference to the Federation's Kashrus Board in a Kashrus Directory issued by the Office, even though products supervised by the Union of Orthodox Hebrew Congregations ("Kedassia") were included. In 1975 further obstruction by Jakobovits and his Beth Din of the proposed merger of kashrus authorities was reported by the Federation's Executive. Two years later, on learning that previous hopes of a merger of the Federation Beth Din with that of the United Synagogue's Chief Rabbi must be abandoned, vacancies on the Federation's Beth Din were filled by the appointment of Rabbi Zalman Alony (then a Dayan in Dublin) as Rosh Beth Din of the Federation, and of Rabbi Dr S. Herman, of the *Ahavath Shalom* Synagogue, as Dayan-Registrar; in the early 1980s Rabbi Yisroel Gukovitzki, who had succeeded his father as Rav of the Springfield Synagogue, was also appointed to the Beth Din, as was Rabbi Gershon Lopian of the *Yeshurun* Synagogue.

Yet, however outstanding were the rabbinic credentials of those appointed to the Federation's Beth Din, its claims to parity of status with that of the United Synagogue and its Chief Rabbi continued to be denied by the United Synagogue and those acting as its agents. Thus, although food manufacturers were allowed by the Kashrus Commission to hold joint licences with the Kedassia organisation, this privilege was not extended to the Federation's Kashrus Board. Nor would the London Board for Shechita permit products manufactured under Federation authority to be sold through its licensees (that is, butcher shops under Shechita Board supervision). "When the laymen of the Shechita Board decided which Beth Din is authoritative and which is not," J. L. Cymerman observed to fellow members of the Federation's Executive in November 1981, "that proved to be the last straw." A year later the Executive approved the commencement of negotiations for the establishment of separate shechita facilities. On 20 May 1984 a Joint Shechita Authority was established by the Federation with the Shechita Board of Luton; shortly afterwards arrangements were agreed for the use of these facilities by the Brighton community.

Within a short space of time the new Joint Shechita Authority succeeded in establishing itself as a most competent communal organisation, offering through a variety of outlets the competition in shechita provision that London Jewry had lacked hitherto. The loss of income to the London Board of Shechita was of course substantial, and proved to be a powerful lever in inducing the United Synagogue to agree to a double compromise. At the beginning of 1987 the United Synagogue, the Spanish & Portuguese congregation and the Federation announced that the London Board of Shechita and the Joint Shechita Authority were to be replaced by a new London Shechita Authority, supervised by a panel of seven rabbis of whom two were to be Federation nominees. Parity of status between the Batei Din of the Federation and that United Synagogue had thus been achieved and, at the same time, the Federation had secured for itself a much greater involvement in shechita than it had had hitherto.

These events were naturally the subject of much attention by the Anglo-Jewish press and, at the level of *haute politique*, were the central preoccupation of Federation policy-makers. But they ought not to be considered in isolation, for they formed but a vivid backcloth against which the Federation reordered its own inner life. The long-standing problem of East End congregations was in large measure solved by the sad but inevitable process of demographics. Ambitious building schemes for East End congregations were gradually forgotten. By the late 1960s the Commercial Road Great Synagogue and what was known as the East London Amalgamated Synagogue, Nelson Street, had emerged as the two major Federation congregations in the East End; in 1968 these merged to form the East London Central Synagogue, which enjoyed constituent status. The Commercial Road site was compulsorily purchased by the Greater London Council. The largest affiliated congregation in the East End was then the Fieldgate Street Great Synagogue, within which the Alie Street community was absorbed in 1969 and the Ezras Chaim Synagogue in 1973.

But although these congregations had large memberships, most of these did not live in the vicinity. In 1970 the total membership of the East London Central was about 1,600; but only 600 lived within a reasonable distance of the synagogue premises. The trustees of East End congregations adopted more reasonable and enlightened attitudes to the disposal of the assets under their stewardship. One example of this deserves special mention. In 1967 the General Council agreed that the gratifying expansion of Ilford Jewry, and the strengthening of Orthodoxy there, demanded the building of a mikvah in the Ilford area. For this purpose the sum of £20,000 was needed, and Lederman was able to announce that those in charge of the assets of the redundant

Dzikower Synagogue & Mikvah (Dunk Street), which had been compulsorily purchased by the Greater London Council, had agreed that the proceeds of the compensation claim might be used for the Ilford project. And so it was that the Ilford Federation Mikvah (Cranbrook Road) was opened, by Morris Lederman in the presence of Immanuel Jakobovits and of the Dayanim of the Federation, on 15 September 1970.

Once familiar landmarks of the Federation in the East End disappeared as East London itself was extensively rebuilt in the 1960s and 1970s. The Jubilee Street Synagogue was closed, its buildings leased to the Association for Jewish Youth. The Canning Town Synagogue was also shut down. Those in Alie Street, Vine Court and Princelet Street were sold, while that in New Road, Whitechapel, was amalgamated with the East London Central. In 1972 the Teesdale Street Synagogue, which had not previously been affiliated to the Federation, agreed to amalgamate with the Bethnal Green Great; the Bethnal Green Synagogue was itself closed in 1984.

In other parts of inner London, too, there was contraction. The Dalston Talmud Torah Synagogue was merged with that of West Hackney, which also (1981) had transferred to it the remaining members of the Montagu Road Beth Hamedrash; the capital assets attaching to the Montagu Road site – amounting to approximately £100,000 – were applied to charitable purposes in Britain and Israel. The Rouel Road Synagogue, Southwark, was purchased by the local borough council, and the proceeds from its sale earmarked for Israel-based projects. The Zionist Federation moved the Clapton Jewish Day School out of its building adjacent to the Clapton Synagogue, which now entered upon a period of prolonged decline (it was formally closed in 2005). The Hillel House School was closed in 1981.

In 1987, as the Federation approached its centenary, there remained but four Federation synagogues in the East End: two constituent (East London Central and Great Garden Street) and two affiliated (the Congregation of Jacob and the Fieldgate Street Great). By 1989 – the year of Morris Lederman's retirement – the major remaining tangible link that the Federation had with the East End was provided by its headquarters. In 1971 the Federation had received unsolicited offers for its premises in Leman Street, which it decided to sell for £131,500 net, roughly £90,000 of which was used to build new offices on the site of a demolished property adjacent to the Great Garden Street Synagogue in Greatorex Street, Whitechapel. The premises, providing twice the capacity of those in Leman Street (and subsequently titled "Morris Lederman House") were opened in 1974.

The construction of a new headquarters coincided with and perhaps helped point to the need for a searching reappraisal of the Federation's organisation and structure. In November 1974, in the wake of the general inflation the UK was then experiencing, the Executive felt it necessary to ask for Burial Society contributions to be increased by 10 (new) pence per week, to meet increased salary costs and to help fund a non-contributory pension fund for officers

Fieldgate Street Great Synagogue, 2006

and staff. The weekly contribution to the Burial Society had already (August 1973) been increased by 5p to meet the needs of the Talmud Torah Council. Another increase so soon was bound to arouse some criticism. A further cause for concern was the size of the Federation's overdraft, which in 1973 stood at £308, 647. Old animosities between affiliated and constituent synagogues were rekindled. In fact, partly due to the aggressive pursuit by head office of tax rebates in respect of covenants taken out by members of constituent synagogues, these synagogues were as a group now producing surpluses that totalled £7,459 for the year 1974; but in that year the *accumulated* net deficits of the constituent synagogues amounted to £44,174 (of which £12,213 pertained to the *Ohel Shem* and £15,162 to the *Shomrei Hadath*).

To judge the viability of congregations solely in terms of financial profit and loss is certainly misguided. A substantial part of the bank overdraft had originated in an ambitious scheme to rebuild the *Yeshurun* Synagogue, which was without doubt a lively and growing community; the Federation was right to advance the funds needed, which were well spent. But overdrafts cannot be carried indefinitely without some reduction. In March 1975 Lederman informed the Executive that, on the advice of the Federation's bankers, interest charged on loans to individual synagogues would be passed on to those synagogues. Although the argument was put that this was justifiable on the grounds that the Federation was merely acting as a guarantor, and although the Beth Din of the Federation had been consulted, the move was widely seen as a retreat from the practice of not charging interest on loans.

There was mounting criticism too of past handling of financial policy. A particular focus of concern was the ill-fated "Israel Project", by which it was envisaged that, in partnership with the Jewish Agency, the Federation would build a *Kirya* in Israel, which would include a hotel for the use of Federation members and a retirement "villa". The Federation had historically been most generous in its Zionist commitment. At the time of the Six-Day War (1967) Federation members had pledged no less than £65,000 in response to Israel's emergency call for funds. An "Aid for Israel" fund had distributed money (over £50,000 in the period 1967-81) donated by Federation members to a wide variety of charities in Israel, both religious and secular. The Federation was represented in the World Zionist Organisation. In 1981 the General Council approved a proposal that donations collected by Federation synagogues in the annual *Kol Nidre* Appeal on *Yom Kippur* would no longer be handed over to the Joint Israel Appeal (in the administration of which the Federation had come to have very little say), but would instead be earmarked for specific projects; the first beneficiary of this policy was the Laniado Hospital at Kiryat Zanz, Netanya, which benefited handsomely in this way through the donation of equipment and the support of services.

The "Israel Project" was, however, frankly misconceived, for there was little to suggest that an excursion into the world of real-estate in Israel was either desirable or desired. By 1971 some £60,000 had been collected for the project through a levy on members. On grounds of cost the original scheme was abandoned, but instead the Armon Hotel, also in Netanya, was purchased (1971) for £120,000, to be used (it was said) as permanent accommodation for retired Federation members and as holiday accommodation. The demand simply did not exist. By August 1973 Lederman was admitting to the General Council that "there had been some error of judgment in the planning of the Israel Project", and in 1976 he revealed that there had been "some difficulty in disposing of a sufficient number of apartments to cover running costs". By 1979 the Hotel was running at a profit, but only because of the presence of a large number of permanent residents, only one of whom was a Federation member. In 1984 it was decided that the Hotel should be sold.

But beyond specific instances of poor decision-making, what became of increasing concern at headquarters were two trends which – it seemed – could not be reversed, at least in the foreseeable future. The first was the decline in membership, which in 1975 stood at about 10,000 (6,000 in constituent synagogues and 4,000 in affiliated congregations). The second was the undeniable fact that this membership was an ageing one. While the number of centres maintained by the Talmud Torah Council had declined to 13 – the combined rolls of which did not exceed 600 – the average age of Burial Society members was then around 65 years; a number of synagogues, especially in the East End, had indeed become mere collection-centres for Burial Society contributions.

Some optimists argued that these trends merely mirrored those being experienced by British Jewry as a whole at this time: British Jewry was contracting in size and acquiring at the same time a surfeit of senior citizens. But the experience of the Federation was wholly disproportionate: for whereas the Jewish communities of the UK were contracting at the rate of about one per cent per annum in the late 1970s, membership of the Federation was apparently falling by about four times this rate. In March 1975 the Honorary Officers, recognising the need for action, established a Sub-Committee on Organisation & Structure, with Lieutenant-Colonel Michael Sack, of the Tottenham Hebrew Congregation, as its Secretary.

In its final report (adopted by the Executive on 15 December 1976), the Sack Sub-Committee pointed especially to a lack of financial control over the budgets of constituent synagogues, some of which were found to have "no idea as to which Members are in arrears". But the central finding of the Sub-Committee was that the bulk of the Federation membership simply could not afford to pay contributions at a level necessary to finance improvements in the services the Federation ought to be offering its congregants. The truth was that whatever economies might be made, the membership as a whole now appeared to be too small to permit any large-scale redevelopment. One effect of this was that the Federation found great difficulty in offering attractive salaries to Dayanim, Ministers and Chazanim. Some Rabbis of high calibre who were persuaded to enter the service of the Federation – such as Dayan Dovid Kaplin – were attracted away by the higher salaries they could command elsewhere. In 1976, two years after he had joined the Federation's Beth Din,

Kaplin left to join that of the United Synagogue. When Dayan Fisher retired as *Rav Rashi* in 1980 he was not replaced.

At the centre of the Federation was its leadership, whose advanced years were only too evident at the centenary celebrations of 1987. And at the centre of this leadership stood Morris Lederman. In the spring of 1989 he announced his retirement. Tragically it had been forced upon him.

Then in his 82nd year, Lederman had filled the office of Federation President almost without a break since 1951. He had matured into a cunning, street-wise communal politician, ruthlessly charming to his friends and charmingly ruthless to his enemies. Against all the odds he had achieved what must have seemed the impossible in 1951: to preserve – indeed, enhance – the Federation's independence during its long and apparently terminal decline. In the 1980s the Federation was still claiming a membership of around 10,000, a figure that was certainly on the optimistic side (in 1992 the actual figure was nearer 7,000). The United Synagogue had long wished to extinguish the Federation's existence. Yet, with its own Beth Din, separate

Dayan Berkovits in the early 1990s, soon after the Federation moved its head office from Greatorex Street in the East End, to Hendon NW4

marriage authorisation office and separate *kashrut* operation, the Federation had, under Lederman's leadership, bravely defied all its detractors.

In 1988 Lederman had indeed pulled off a major coup, by enticing to London a dynamic, American-born rabbi, to become *Rosh Beth Din* – chief judge – of the Federation's ecclesiastical court. Dayan Yisroel Yaacov Lichtenstein, a graduate of New York State University, brought to the religious leadership of the Federation an Orthodox modernity which was sadly lacking in its counterpart in the United Synagogue, and which the Union of Orthodox Hebrew Congregations (within which the American Dayan was himself very much *persona grata*) would never have dared espouse. Two years later Rabbi Berel Berkovits (1949-2005), formerly a law lecturer at the University of Buckingham, defected from the United Synagogue to the Federation, to become a Dayan sitting alongside Rabbi Lichtenstein. The Federation could now boast the most intellectually distinguished Beth Din in the UK.

But although the presidency of the Federation was meant to be an honorary rather than an executive position, Morris Lederman had, somehow, managed to extract from its coffers substantial payments of expenses, and had, somehow, managed to persuade others to agree to his being able to draw a pension (amounting to £15,000 per annum in 1990 and 1991) from its Burial Society funds upon retirement. These payments (which ceased in 1993) might have been forgiven – for had not Lederman given his life to the service of the Federation? – but when members of the Federation's Executive received the audited accounts for 1987 and 1988 they were shocked to discover that the auditors had prefaced them with a series of damning qualifications, amounting to a charge of gross mismanagement – and worse – against Lederman and some of his former associates.

All in all, sums totalling around £1.6 millions, derived in part from the London Talmud Torah Council, in part from the sale of five redundant affiliated synagogues (Alie Street, Canning Town, Vine Court, *Ezras Chaim* and the Cavell Street site), but also including moneys earmarked for "The Israel

Charity Project" (which had in turn been funded, without authorisation, from the Burial Society) had been diverted to accounts in the Channel Islands and Israel; these monies belonged to the Federation, but in some cases had been deposited under the names of Morris Lederman and members of his immediate family.

Following Lederman's retirement, the presidency of the Federation fell by election to Arnold Cohen (1936-2016), a Federation Treasurer since 1985, the much-respected head of an accountancy firm, and an alumnus of Gateshead Yeshiva. Cohen appointed a senior member of the Federation, solicitor Harold Ragol-Levy (d.2007), to head an investigation. From time to time Ragol-Levy reported to the Federation's Executive, indicating that discussions of an unspecified nature were in train with Lederman, members of his family and "other persons". In return for his co-operation in pinpointing the location of moneys belonging to the Federation, Lederman and his family were able to reach agreements with it by which moneys were to be repaid, in instalments and with interest, whilst property belonging to him was transferred to Federation ownership. Some moneys were indeed repaid; but the full amount owing was never recovered.

Arnold Cohen zl when he became President of the Federation in 1989

The Ragol-Levy report (November 1992) concluded on this sombre note:

We are not satisfied that the acts of Mr. M. Lederman were always in the best interests of the Federation of Synagogues or had the proper authority of his fellow Honorary Officers. Nor are we satisfied that he always fully informed his fellow Honorary Officers, the members of the Executive or the Council of his actions or kept adequate records as he should. Mr. M. Lederman transferred funds out of the control of the elected Honorary Officers of the Federation by appointing both of his sons and one of his grandsons as signatories who could sign alone on certain Ancillary Fund bank accounts and arranging for them to transfer funds properly belonging to those Ancillary Funds of the Federation of Synagogues to off-shore companies over which he or the Federation had no formal control.

Lederman had indeed served the Federation well. But at the same time he had robbed its members to serve his own personal ends. What he had done did indeed amount, in Arnold Cohen's words, to "the rape of the Federation".

Yet, against all the odds, the Federation was about to enter upon a period of renewed growth. In part this was due to a most fortuitous – some would say God-given – discovery.

We noted in Chapter Three that in 1936 Morry Davis, the Federation's contentious and autocratic third president, had arranged for it to purchase, for burial purposes and at an advantageous price, waterlogged land at Rainham, Essex, deemed unsuitable for farming. Like everything else that Davis did, this initiative was mired (almost literally) in controversy, partly on account of the distance of the new burial ground from the bulk of the Federation's membership and partly on account of the expense incurred in drainage works. But Davis had the last laugh. In 2008 Havering Aggregates, a local mineral extraction company, purchased from the Federation a ten-year lease which gave it the right to extract gravel from those areas of land

(and they were considerable) not then currently in use for burial purposes. As a result, during the period 2008 to 2018 inclusive, sums totalling at least £1.4 millions will have accrued to the Federation in the form of extraction royalties. These revenues, plus significant supervision fees levied by the Federation in respect of kosher restaurants and food manufacturing outlets, have transformed the Federation's balance sheet and enabled it to flourish and indeed grow.

But we need to remember that this windfall could not have been foreseen when Arnold Cohen became President. His tenure of office (1989 – 2001) might well have seen a merger, perforce, with the United Synagogue. But this – though certainly the subject of private, unofficial discussion from time to time – never happened.

Much of Cohen's time, and that of his fellow Honorary Officers (including Treasurer Alan Finlay, a solicitor, who served as Federation President from 2001 until 2014) was inevitably occupied with the need to confront the financial and bureaucratic disarray that was evident even before Lederman had stepped down. On 15 June 1989, in reporting to Council that Gerald

Current Federation offices in Hendon, 2016

Kushner (by background an accountant) had been appointed as "Head of Administration" in succession to Michael Goldman (who however continued for some years as Clerk to the Federation's Beth Din), Cohen felt the need to draw attention also to the lamentable physical state of Head Office, whose resources and equipment were out of date and which lacked even a fax machine. Scarcely less urgent was the need to relocate Head Office away from an East End whose Jewish clientèle was fast disappearing. A site was purchased at 65 Watford Way, central Hendon (opened May 1992), with superior office accommodation (into which the Burial Society and Beth Din were moved, as well as the Federation's kashrus division) a small synagogue which could also double as an assembly room for Council meetings, and ample space for the appurtenances of a modern administrative headquarters, including digital media and communications. Morris Lederman House, Greatorex Street, was put on the market – though its sale was not concluded until 1997.

The presidencies of Cohen and Finlay might have been totally overwhelmed by the need simply to keep the Federation afloat, figuratively speaking. In fact, although mere survival was certainly an early priority, these decades were actually ones of consolidation and then of renewed growth. We need to ask how this was achieved, and we need to understand why.

Arnold Cohen and his fellow Honorary Officers were able to bring order into the financial chaos that had characterised the final years of the Lederman presidency. For some years the Federation was kept financially sound only through the sale of properties, and interest of moneys kept on deposit at the House of Rothschild. The administration and – more importantly – the funds of the London Talmud Torah Council and the Burial Society were transferred wholly to the Federation. For some years, unsurprisingly, the deficit position of the Federation continued to worsen. In 1992 this deficit stood at £275,000. On 18 May 1993 Cohen told the Council that the deficit had grown to £355,000. Burial fees were raised, but since more than half the members of the Burial Society were then over 70 years of age, and since a significant number of these would not or could not afford the increase, Cohen and his colleagues were frank enough to admit that the totality of the hoped-for additional income (£95,000 per annum) was unlikely to be realised. So, a one-time levy of £52 per Federation member (whether or not the member was within the Burial scheme, and excluding senior citizens) was imposed, while all staff salaries were frozen.

Paradoxically, however, it was precisely in these years of severe financial constraint that the seeds of future growth were sown. Under the leadership of Rabbi (later Dayan) Moshe Elzas, the Federation's Kashrus division became a significant source of much-needed income; revenue from this division rose from £24,000 in the last eight months of 1995 to £55,000 in the first eight months of the following year. At the same time, Dayan Lichtenstein's expertise had proved invaluable to the reconstituted London Shechita Board, which from 1994 began to make annual payments (initially £10,000) to the Federation in respect of the shechita-related services rendered by its Dayanim. In 1997 the Executive agreed to the sale of three of the Federation's fourteen constituent synagogues (Neasden, Woolwich and South Hackney). Of the remaining affiliated congregations (also fourteen, none of which were,

Dayan Elzas (left) and Dayan Lichtenstein, 2016

legally, under Federation control) there was a parallel rationalisation, since those (roughly half) that were not able to muster a *minyan* even on the Sabbath were gradually forced to close their doors.

During 1996 the Federation began to benefit from moneys recovered from the Lederman family; these funds were earmarked for the construction of new synagogues in the Greater London conurbation. In March 1996 Cohen was able to report that the Federation's underlying deficit had been reduced to around £60,000, and later that year he revealed to Council that the Federation's capital reserves were of the order of £1 million. A new synagogue was opened at Croydon. The facilities at the Rainham cemetery were upgraded. Plans were drafted for the establishment of a Federation *kehilla* in Elstree. In 1997 the Federation made a grant of £1,000 to the South London Mikvah. The following year Rabbi H. Vogel was appointed by the

Federation Sign, c1992

Federation as Student Chaplain for universities and colleges in the south-east of England, and in 1998 the Federation announced that it had agreed to sponsor the Jewish chaplaincy at the University of Manchester for three years at £15,000 per annum.

The Federation's involvement in pastoral work in England's higher-education sector was not simply, however, a matter of money. It reflected also the determination of Cohen and his team to re-establish the status of the Federation within the world of British Jewry. Confrontation with the United Synagogue was central to this strategy. Reporting to the General Council (7 December 1993) on the failure of talks with the United Synagogue on the possibility of merging the *Batei Din* of the two bodies, Cohen observed that the Honorary Officers of the United Synagogue "were not really interested in a merger; they were only interested in swallowing the Federation up". The dialogue was therefore brought to an end. The Beth Din of the Federation was aggressively marketed as a prestigious ecclesiastical court of the last resort for Orthodox Jews throughout the world. In 1998, following an interview that Dayan Berkovits had given on BBC Radio 4, it began to hear cases brought by non-Jewish litigants.

We might also note that Berkovits's input had also been central to the successful insertion into what became the Family Law Act of 1996 of an amendment empowering a civil court to require a divorcing Jewish couple to declare that they had taken the necessary action to have their religious marriage dissolved as a condition precedent to the granting of a civil divorce. This much-needed contribution to the solution of the plight of the aguna– the "chained" wife who cannot remarry because her recalcitrant husband refuses to issue a *get* – was not strictly speaking a Federation initiative. But there was no doubt that the Federation's input – through the efforts of Dayanim Berkovits and Lichtenstein – had proved pivotal to Parliament's endorsement of it.

Cohen and his team had, meanwhile, further distanced the Federation from the concept of "centrist" Orthodoxy, as represented by the United

Synagogue. In 1994 he announced that although both constituent and affiliated congregations were free to seek representation on the Board of Deputies if they wished, "Head Office" would no longer be represented on it. In 1989 the Federation had declined to take part in the process – instigated by the United Synagogue – of choosing Jonathan Sacks to succeed to Immanuel Jakobovits as Chief Rabbi of the United Hebrew Congregations. Twenty-five years later Alan Finlay was to announce that the Federation would play no part in the election of a successor to Sacks (Ephraim Mirvis).

In June 2001 Arnold Cohen retired from the Presidency, together with his Vice-Presidents, Jonathan Winegarten and Jeffrey Gitlin. He bequeathed to his successor a Federation that was much stronger than that which he had inherited in 1989. But he also bequeathed three problems that he and his team had not been able to solve: the Federation's increasingly outdated constitution; female representation at local and head-office levels; and the provision of a cemetery in north-west London.

Dating from 1947, the constitution as it then existed stipulated that the General Council was the Federation's supreme governing body. No decision of any importance – for example the buying or selling of property – no matter how confidential or time-sensitive, could strictly speaking be taken without the Council's prior approval. It had also become apparent that, notwithstanding any resolution to the contrary that may have been passed by the Council, the

Alan Finlay

Federation's ultimate trustees were in fact the individual Council members, who bore this ultimate responsibility and the personal legal liability that accompanied it. Nor did the 1947 constitution make any provision for the representation on it of female Federation members.

The issue of female representation – the second of the problems that remained unsolved in 2001 - had scarcely existed in 1947, but, reflecting pressures emanating from the wider world, it had grown in intensity during the Cohen presidency. It was of course basically a *halachic* matter. In individual Federation synagogues women had always played a prominent part, but rather on the social and educational side, never as part of the management structure. An Association of Ladies' Guilds had been established – belatedly – in 1969. But in July 1977 Morris Lederman had been obliged to report that the *Rav Rashi* - Dayan Fisher – had ruled that it would not be permissible for lady members (even if members in their own right) to be granted the eligibility to vote at elections for synagogue honorary officers or boards of management, or as delegates to the General Council. Some years later the Federation's Beth Din refused to permit a constituent synagogue to elect a woman as a member of the Board of Deputies.

These strictures were gradually relaxed under the authority of Dayan Lichtenstein, who in December 2008 issued an authoritative *P'sak Din* on the role of women in the Federation. The issue of female representation at the Board of Deputies was left to individual congregations. More importantly, lady members of both constituent and affiliated congregations were permitted to elect women as members of their individual boards of management and to appoint women as their representatives on Council; in due course Mrs Barbara Cohen became the first female chairperson of a Federation synagogue (the affiliated Loughton congregation). In 2013-14, during the last full year of the Finlay presidency, and following discussion of a lengthy report on constitutional reform grounded in the deliberations of a working party chaired by Rabbi Jeffrey Cohen, a new Constitution (approved by the Charity

Commission) was overwhelmingly adopted. The Council is now, in effect, an advisory body to the trustees (the Federation President, two Vice-Presidents, two Treasurers and two Treasurers of the Burial Society), whom it elects. While the trustees must be male, every affiliated and constituent synagogue is permitted to "appoint" female delegates, who thus become full Council members.

The matter of cemetery provision had preoccupied the deliberations of Council for several decades. Whilst it was true that the acreage at Rainham was much more than adequate for the needs of the Burial Society in the foreseeable future, its location was regarded as problematic even for those Federation members who lived in the eastern and north-eastern parts of the capital. In 1998 farmland had been purchased virtually adjacent to Northwood Hills station, Harrow; but planning permission to convert the farm into a cemetery was never forthcoming. It was not until September 2014 that chartered accountant Andrew Cohen, who had in December 2013 succeeded Alan Finlay as Federation President, was able to announce the successful purchase (for £1.6 million) of land designated for burial purposes in Edgware.

The quarter-century that followed the end of the Lederman presidency thus saw the Federation modernise itself. It has also, unashamedly, taken

Andrew Cohen, 2016

advantage of divisions that have appeared in other Orthodox communities (especially the Union of Orthodox Hebrew Congregations) to grow its own membership. At the time of writing (January 2015) the Federation comprises nine affiliated congregations and fourteen constituents, which include the *Beis Hamedrash Nishmas Yisroel* in central Hendon and the *Ohr Yerushalayim* in Salford – the Federation's first constituent outside Greater London. Two other constituents, Ilford and Finchley Central, have moved into new premises. At the beginning of 2015 the Federation's Burial Society had almost 2,900 subscribing members on its books, representing perhaps 9,000 souls; to these should be added those in membership of Federation synagogues, but not its Burial Society, so that total membership (in one form or another) of the Federation was then probably in excess of 12,000. Reports of the Federation's imminent demise – which circulated freely and mischievously as recently as a decade ago – do indeed seem wildly premature. How are we to account for this?

Because of its small size, the Federation permits its members a much more active involvement in communal affairs than is the case in larger, impersonal communities, and is more receptive to its needs. At the same time, within the umbrella of strict Torah Orthodoxy, the Federation's internal structure offers more freedom to individual congregations to shape the daily routine of synagogal life according to their own traditions and customs. This underpinning of an independent but totally authentic Orthodoxy is surely the Federation's greatest strength. But other strengths flow from it. A Strategy Review ordered by Alan Finlay reported thus in January 2013:

> *The Federation is a dynamic, forward-looking organisation that is proud to empower today's independent, Orthodox communities – enabling them to achieve their individual goals and objectives and, thereby, helping them to promote their love of Torah, fellowship and Israel.*

Clearly this statement positions The Federation as an 'empowering entity', delivering a genuinely 'federal' system that puts the individual community first – enabling their independence within a supportive and meaningful framework. The report went on to stress that the Federation "must focus its energies and activities on servicing (and being seen to service) the needs of its communities – helping them to grow and realise their potential in spiritual, social and membership/financial terms."

If it does so, the Federation can surely look forward to a constructive and successful future.

INDEX

#0127 - 090718 - C0 - 210/148/11 - PB - DID2243601